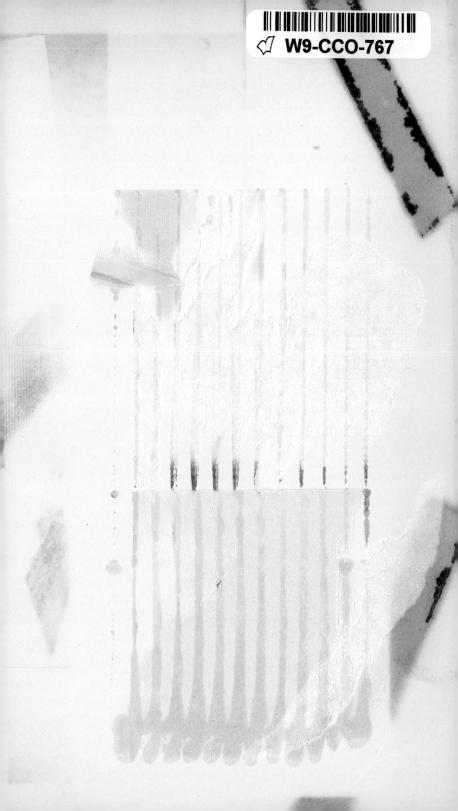

Words into rhythm

THE CLARK LECTURES 1971–1972

# Words into rhythm

*English speech rhythm in verse and prose*

### D. W. HARDING

EMERITUS PROFESSOR OF PSYCHOLOGY
IN THE UNIVERSITY OF LONDON

CAMBRIDGE UNIVERSITY PRESS

CAMBRIDGE

LONDON · NEW YORK · MELBOURNE

Published by the Syndics of the Cambridge University Press
The Pitt Building, Trumpington Street, Cambridge CB2 1RP
Bentley House, 200 Euston Road, London NW1 2DB
32 East 57th Street, New York, NY 10022, USA
296 Beaconsfield Parade, Middle Park, Melbourne 3206, Australia

First published 1976

Printed in Great Britain by
W & J Mackay Limited, Chatham

*Library of Congress Cataloguing in Publication Data*
Harding, Denys Clement Wyatt, 1906–
Words into rhythm
(The Clark lectures, 1971–1972)
Includes bibliographical references and index.
1. English language–Rhythm. 2. Rhythm–Psychological aspects.
I. Title. II. Series: The Clark lectures, Trinity College,
Cambridge University, 1971–1972.
PE1559.H3   426   76–7805
ISBN 0 521 21267 7

# Contents

Preface                                                vii

1   The nature of rhythm                                  1
2   Speech and the rhythm of verse                       17
3   Metrical set and rhythmical variation                31
4   Effects of deviation from metre                      45
5   Rhythms of irregular verse                           59
6   Unsatisfactory rhythms                               72
7   Expressive effects of rhythm in verse                85
8   Modes of energy release in rhythm                    98
9   Rhythms in prose                                     116
10  Expressive effects of prose rhythm                   134
11  The gist                                             152

    References                                           159
    Index                                                163

# Preface

I am most grateful to the Council of Trinity College, Cambridge, for the opportunity of giving these lectures, with the stimulus it offered to complete a piece of work I had had in hand for some time. I received great kindness and practical help from Mr Leo Salingar during the course.

The five lectures have been revised for publication, chiefly by a closer examination of one or two problems and the addition of further examples and demonstrations. In giving the lectures I greatly appreciated the encouragement of an audience who were willing to follow the discussion of material much of which had to be presented by word of mouth and was not easy to take in by ear.

# The nature of rhythm

The word rhythm is given such astonishingly wide application that if we could believe it really meant something, and the same thing in different contexts, we could accept it as a master-key for innumerable locks. Bridging the rhythm of marching feet to the rhythm of the universe – taking in, on the way, the rhythm of the seasons, the circadian rhythm of animal activities, the rhythm of work, primitive and industrial, and all the rhythms found or talked of in literature and most of the other arts – the word becomes a vast unsupported span. It may seem pedantic to want a definition, but the alternative is the endlessly extending use of the word to cover more and more processes, usually distinct from one another, occasionally even incompatible. Thus for some of the early industrial psychologists a rhythmical movement was one that flowed in smooth curves rather than having angular changes of direction, while for others a continuous circular movement precluded rhythm. The 'rhythm of the seasons' refers to regular timing and recurrence, or periodicity. In the 'rhythm of night and day' the regular alternation of phases is the main idea, their timing (at least in our latitude) being in continuous gradual change. The 'rhythm of life' and the 'rhythm of the universe' seem to be uplifting ways of referring to a coordination of component processes and perhaps an ordered progression of stages.

Vague and various and metaphorical uses of the word need not be objectionable in ordinary speech, where the context makes the speaker's intention as clear as need be. But in any attempt at literal statement it must be preferable to use the more accurate terms that the language already provides for these discriminable senses: terms such as ordering, structure, coordination, progression, regular alternation, smoothness, periodicity.

For some writers, however, the faintly romantic or emotional overtones of the word rhythm seem to offer a welcome escape from the rigour of rational statement. Herbert Read (1943) quotes approvingly from the verbal elaborations with which Dalcroze supported his system of eurhythmics:

Life, in effect, is itself a rhythm, that is a continuous succession of multiple units, forming an indivisible whole. Individuality may also be regarded as a rhythm, for the combination of its faculties, many of them conflicting, constitute[s] an entity. But every life and every work of art that conforms only to the idiosyncrasies of the individual is arrhythmic, for the rhythm of art and life demands the fusion of all traits of character and temperament. (p. 66)

Susanne Langer (1953) casts her net equally wide when she claims that music organizes feeling in a way that gives insight into the 'subjective unity of experience; and this it does by the same principle that organizes physical existence into a biological design – rhythm' (p. 126). This – fairly typical of the loosely comprehensive use – makes 'rhythm' cover the multifarious processes guided by genetic coding, from the myelinization of nerve fibres to eye-watering, vocal utterance, walking, resistance to infection, aggression, fear, pubescence, social interaction, and so indefinitely on. All she seems to mean is that some kind of design can be identified in the life of an animal, and rhythm too is some kind of design. Used in such ways, the word is only a broad, reassuring gesture. A reader satisfied with that would do well to skip this chapter, in which a closer definition of the term is offered and a more matter of fact account given of the nature of rhythm.

But in literature need we trouble to define rhythm clearly or try to establish what effects it has and how they come about? In a reader's purely private commerce with a poem it probably makes no difference whether or not he knows, in an abstract way, anything at all about rhythm; he need only read sensitively and let the rhythm do its work. The situation changes if he once starts discussing the poem, drawing attention to the aspects he finds specially satisfying or feels doubtful about, seeking companionship in his enjoyment, trying to benefit from the insights of other readers. Whether in formal criticism or ordinary conversational exchanges, once the discussion gets beyond simple exclamations of pleasure or dislike we can only benefit by having a clear meaning for the terms we use and knowing what effects can reasonably be attributed to this or that feature of the work.

Rhythm, especially in poetry, has been given immense significance by literary critics, at times credited with particular effects, at others taken as a sign of some more general quality of the writing. In an early work of criticism F. R. Leavis (1932) commended the positive assurance of a poem he quoted, and added

The grounds for this positive note are not matter for debate – at any rate here. The assurance justifies itself; those rhythms are not to be dealt with by argument. (p. 208)

More recently Rachel Trickett (1967) in her study of Augustan verse quotes a passage from Dryden, *The Hind and the Panther*:

> 'Tis nothing thou hast giv'n, then add thy tears
> For a long race of unrepenting years:
> 'Tis nothing yet; yet all thou hast to give,
> Then add those *may-be* years thou hast to live.
> Yet nothing still: then poor, and naked come,
> Thy father will receive his unthrift home,
> And thy blest Saviour's bloud discharge the mighty sum.

And her comment is that 'The rhythms of the final lines in the passage quoted above have an emotional intensity that recalls Donne...' We might agree that something in the mood and the estimate of himself recall Donne, but we might still wonder whether it is the rhythm of the lines that conveys the intense emotion; the question is hard to answer when the rhythm is inextricably bound up with the sense of the words.

Again, L. C. Knights (1976) in an illuminating study of Blake's early poems writes of 'My silks and fine array'

If proof of poetic genius were wanted it could be found in the subtly changing rhythms of this poem. No account in terms of shifts from iambic to trochaic, reversed stresses, and so on, can do it justice; all one needs to do is to see how tone and rhythm define meanings that could not otherwise be put into words. (p. 56)

Having made this general claim for the importance of the rhythm he points to one of its particular effects:

> My silks and fine array,
>     My smiles and languish'd air,
> By love are driv'n away;
>     And mournful lean Despair
> Brings me yew to deck my grave:
> Such end true lovers have.

In the fifth line, he says, 'The plangent tone that comes with the shift of rhythm. . . has just that shade of self-conscious self-awareness that warns us against identifying with the speaker, who unconsciously reveals, as well as expresses, herself.'

These are representative examples of the importance modern literary criticism attaches to rhythm, and the great potency claimed for it, including the power of conveying very subtle shades of attitude. How it does this, if it does, is a question to consider later. At the moment what must be examined is the nature of the thing to which such power is attributed.

Conventional literary criticism has not been as helpful as one might have hoped. Tillyard (1934) opens a chapter headed 'Rhythm' with the statement 'I use the word "rhythm" in a very wide sense to cover all the effects that the sound of the words commands'. In that case, one wonders, why use the term 'rhythm' at all instead of sticking to the better understood word 'sound'? At the opposite academic extreme, a very different concept of rhythm could be implied, as late as 1965, in a 'casebook' intended for American college students (Gwynn et al., 1965), where the commentary on one poem includes a section headed 'Rhythm':

Although the uniform trimeter seems jingly when it is read aloud, it is actually so varied in two kinds of feet as to barely allow a traditional foot label. With an almost equal number of anapests (31) and iambs (28, plus one truncated iamb beginning line 19), and with an exactly equal number of lines dominated by anapests or iambs, we must label the pattern mixed anapestic-iambic trimeter. (p. 131)

When I first thought about the subject very long ago, I. A. Richards' account in *Principles of Literary Criticism* seemed illuminating and thoroughly satisfying. 'Rhythm' he writes 'and its specialised form, metre, depend upon repetition and expectancy'. He goes on

The expectancy caused by what has gone before, a thing which must be thought of as a very complex tide of neural settings, lowering the threshold for some kinds of stimuli and raising it for others, and the character of the stimulus which does actually come, both play their part. (p. 135)

This still seems true. It becomes less satisfying, however, when you reflect that it applies equally to all perceptual experience that prepares you for something else: the sight of a comfortable arm chair before you sink into it, the smell of toast for breakfast, the crescendo and fading of sound as a jet aircraft goes over, the shade of trees on a hot day. It says too little specifically about rhythm. None the less it was in 1926 a refreshing change from the impression conveyed by a writer like George Saintsbury that rhythm was a system of iambs, trochees, dactyls, anapaests, cretics, amphibrachs, first, second, third and fourth paeons, and so on through the whole erudite labelling. Richards' approach was specially valuable and permanently valuable in its insistence that rhythm was an active process in a responding person.

In psychology this was already a well established view. It had been stated by James Ward, Fellow of Trinity College and Professor of Mental Philosophy who founded the Cambridge school of psychology, and his account (1918) is still an excellent starting point. He gave special attention to the subjective experience we have of a differentiation and grouping in a sequence of sounds which are objectively all alike and follow each other at perfectly regular intervals, the experience, for example, of hearing the ticking of a clock as tick-tock-tick-tock instead of tick-tick-tick-tick. He has no doubt about excluding merely regular repetition from the concept of rhythm. He writes (drawing on the studies of T. L. Bolton, an American psychologist)

What is remarkable is that even a perfectly regular succession of sounds (or touches), qualitatively and quantitatively all alike, a series therefore devoid of all objective rhythm, is nevertheless apprehended by most people as rhythmically grouped – provided the rate lies between the limits of about 0.8″ and 0.14″. The slower of these rates leads to simple groups of two, replaced by groups of four or eight as the rate increases; groups of three and six also occur, though less frequently...With slower rates there was no grouping at all and with faster rates 'simply a periodic intensive change in the series'. (p. 228)

This was the conception of rhythm adopted by psychologists who investigated the subject in the early years of this century, for instance R. MacDougall (1903) and J. B. Miner (1903). They saw rhythmization as a form of unifying activity: a number of sensory impressions that might be merely a sequence can, if rhythmized, be perceived as a unit. Further, the unification is not mediated by other activities such as counting but is an immediate perception, an 'immediate fact of sensory apprehension' (R. MacDougall). In the same way, in visual experience, we have an immediate perception of an octagon or a hexagon – we may need to count the sides in order to label the figure but we experience it as a unit of a particular form without any auxiliary intellectual activity. Moreover in a rhythmical unit the individual sensory impressions are differentiated: some are salient, others subordinate, as in the simple tick-tock of a clock. In contrast, a brief burst of machine-gun fire may be heard as a unit but is not rhythmized; its component sounds are held together only by their nearness in time, not identified and related to each other by different degrees of perceptual salience.

A sequence of sensory impressions which are grasped with perceptual immediacy as a unit and at the same time differentiated among themselves may arise not only from sound but from muscular movement, as they do in dancing, or from movement and sound combined as in playing a musical instrument or speaking, or from imagined speech sounds and movements as in silent reading, or from seen movement as in watching a dancer or observing the climbing pattern of a wave or the stepping pattern of a wading bird at the water's edge. In listening to a speaker we fuse the sounds heard with images of the speech movements that produce them. Whatever sensory mode or modes may be involved, the experience of rhythm is the experience of a perceptually immediate grouping or unity in a sequence of impressions, together with a differentiation of the component members of the group. An important secondary fact, noted by many of the early workers, is that once rhythmization in a certain form has been established it readily recurs in the same form.

Although rhythmizing is an active process, something done to a sequence by the person who perceives it, the particular form of the patterning is generally determined, at least in part, by objective characteristics of the impressions. Only exceptionally, as in listening to a metronome or clock, is the rhythmizing purely subjective. In language it is obviously not. In speaking and listening and reading we are not creating rhythmical patterns at our own sweet will; the basic features of the spoken language control our rhythmizing while we speak, and the rhythms we perceive as listeners or silent readers are guided, and sometimes closely controlled, by objective features of the sound sequences and by the usages of the particular language. (The extent to which the reader has latitude to choose his own variant of the rhythm is a point I want to discuss later.)

The rhythms adopted in typewriting illustrate in a simplified way how the physical features of the medium in which we are making movements help to determine the rhythmical pattern of the movement (Harding, 1933). The expert typist, using all fingers in the orthodox way, establishes for any familiar word (or phrase) a pattern made up of quick runs and slight pauses peculiar to that word, and sticks fairly closely to it whenever the word occurs. By 'pause' I mean an interval between one letter and the next which is very slightly longer than the extremely brief intervals between letters that form a run. With a skilled typist working rapidly the rhythm of runs and pauses can rarely be identified by ear and has to be recorded mechanically, but then it shows up clearly and can be measured and accurately described. There are differences among typists in the degree to which the pattern is emphasized and the consistency with which it is maintained on recurrences of the word, but in the main the pattern of each word is determined simply by the layout of the keyboard and its relation to the possibilities of manual movement; in particular, successive strokes follow one another more rapidly if they involve an alternation of the two hands than they do if different fingers of the same hand are used in succession. The practised typist thus creates runs and pauses quite independent of pronounceable syllables. For example, 'capacity' runs c apa city, 'latent' runs la t ent, and 'strident' runs s t rid ent; and words like 'movement', 'statement' etc. are not given the division suggested by spelling but end with a rapid group, *ement*. There are other factors of less importance than the successive use of the same hand or alternate hands, especially the time needed for the long reach with the same hand between the top and bottom rows; so that 'minimum', for instance, has to be a fairly slow regular plodding. (In good typing the rhythms are expressed solely in runs and pauses, without differences of force – which would produce uneven impressions.)

In speech similarly the physical machinery involved in pronouncing particular sequences of sound establishes *some* patterning in the form of speed variations among syllables. But a more important source of patterning is provided not by the mechanical but by the customary features of the spoken language, in English notably accentuation. Divisions of sense, whether indicated by punctuation or not, add another element in the patterning of the flow of utterance. Over and above these are differences among speakers, not only in spontaneous speech but also in reading where, even in the absence of accidental hesitations, there are great differences in speed changes, length of pauses, elisions, lingerings, and degree of contrast between strongly and lightly stressed syllables. Whether verse adds another factor to determine rhythmical grouping, or only selects and organizes the natural rhythms of speech, is a question for later discussion.

If we ask what in more detail are the features that determine or suggest rhythm in English we dislodge a stone that will bring an avalanche of diverse answers on us. Differences of loudness, differences of stress (which need not be the same), differences of syllable length, pitch differences, pauses preceding or following a syllable, position in a time pattern, all of these have been suggested, and some disputed, by phoneticians and workers in allied disciplines. Moreover these various features of speech interact and modify each other in such a subtle and intricate way that the contribution of each to a total speech pattern may be almost impossible to distinguish. But though an analytic description can be almost defeatingly difficult, the upshot in experience is always much simpler – an awareness of different degrees of salience among the syllables that make up the unit of rhythm. The relative salience of a syllable can be determined by one or more of the objective features of the sound, and some of these are influenced by the sense. But usually in English a difference of stress is the main thing that gives a syllable its relative prominence in the rhythm unit, and some degree of pause is the thing that marks the end of one unit and the beginning of the next.

The mechanism of stress is explained by David Abercrombie (1965) in one of his succinct and lucid essays ('A phonetician's view of verse structure'). The air stream producing sounds comes in chest pulses (dependent on the intercostal muscles), each pulse constituting a syllable; in addition there occur less frequent stress pulses, more powerful contractions of the breathing muscles which coincide with one of the chest pulses and cause a greater and more sudden rise in air pressure.

In spoken language the division of the flow of sound into rhythmical units is an essential part of the skill of speaking, and a grasp of those units is equally necessary for listening with comprehension. As we all know, you can have a reading knowledge of a foreign language and still find the native speaker incomprehensible because the runs and pauses, the elisions and the lingerings, occur at unexpected points and create different divisions from those suggested by the printed words. In an accentual language like English a foreign speaker – for instance an Indian accustomed to an unaccented vernacular – can be strangely baffling simply by failing to make the expected stress differentiations among the syllables even though he pronounces them correctly. In fact W. Stannard Allen (1954), in a book called *Living English Speech: Stress and Intonation Practice for Foreign Students*, suggests that poorly enunciated words conforming to the right rhythm will often be more intelligible than correctly pronounced words wrongly rhythmized.

His exercises show that a great deal about speech rhythm can be conveyed by indicating merely the main stresses among the syllables of a word or phrase. Other specialists in language resort to ever more complicated notations in the effort to register the details of what goes on in speech. The fact seems to be that if we know English as a native language we can get a long way by indicating the main stress in each rhythm unit and the points of pause, sometimes well marked, sometimes minimal, which occur between rhythm units. Within the broad pattern of the rhythm there will be subtler shadings provided by such things as the length of syllables and different degrees of subordinate stress (such as the Trager and Smith (1951) notation records). Generally the context and sense will tell a native user of the language what subordinate stresses are called for (as well as what intonation or pattern of pitch). But an indication of the main stresses and the points of pause can often be useful in showing which of alternative rhythms one is choosing in a verse line or a phrase.

A rather difficult problem concerns the effect of a syllable's duration on the rhythm unit in which it occurs. It is tempting to simplify the complicated and controversial question of the stimulus features suggesting particular rhythms by reducing them all to stress and the time between stresses. This was the line taken by William Thomson (1923) in the monumental work that was so far ahead of current thinking in his day. He believed that only the onset or point of main force in each syllable and the time intervals between onsets were relevant to rhythm. Much later the same simplification was attempted by J. B. Davies (1971) who argued that the duration of a sound has no bearing on the rhythm of the sequence in which it occurs. He saw rhythm

as an order which the listener imposes upon sequences of tonal elements solely on the basis of their relative intensity, and their relative times of onset. It is argued also that changes in duration of elements *in no way* change rhythm, provided that accent and relative time of onset do not change. (p. 561)

He noted, in support of this view, that to clap the rhythm of a tune played on an instrument is a meaningful task, although in the tune as played all tones have duration.

Tempting though it is, this view is almost certainly an over-simplification. In the morse code, for example, it seems reasonable to consider each letter as a unit or sub-unit of rhythm. Here there are no differences of intensity in the component sounds, and the variations in the time of onset of each sound are not enough to mark all the differences that have to be perceived. It seems unreal to deny that the difference in length between a dot and a dash is relevant to the rhythm of a letter. Presumably Davies would argue that in

... --- ...

the dashes are taken, rhythmically, as if each were a dot followed by a longer pause than a true dot. But the times of onset of the sounds are the same in the two letters

... and ..-

and to discriminate between them we are bound to perceive the longer duration of the dash. There seems no reason to deny the term 'rhythm' to the sound pattern of which this is an essential feature.

A similar conclusion is reached by looking at the stress patterns used by W. Stannard Allen to indicate the rhythms of spoken English. He uses simply a small and a large symbol to stand for the lightly stressed and the strongly stressed syllables, thus:

OooO    send him away; hardly enough; pouring with rain.

But suitable as this is for Stannard Allen's workaday purposes with foreign students it conveys a wrong impression here and there by giving the same rhythm to phrases which, because of the duration of some syllables, sound different; thus, oOooo is made to cover not only 'it's necessary' and 'the railway station' but also 'a beautiful one', 'in spite of it all', 'I asked if I could'. It would not be fully satisfactory to use the same rhythm for 'it's necessary' and 'in spite of it all' because that would give too much salience to the last syllable of 'necessary'. Trager and Smith might get round the difficulty with a secondary or tertiary stress on 'all', but it looks more probable that 'all' receives a little more salience than 'ry' because it takes longer to say. Whatever the precise contributory factors, there seems to be an undeniable rhythmical difference between some words that have the same accentual pattern, say 'typical' and 'somnolent'; and the length of the sounds would appear to be at least one of the factors. The difference is similar to that between letters in the morse code, though with the addition of differential stress in verbal phrases:

.⁻... for 'it's necessary';

.⁻..— for 'in spite of it all'.

In fact Stannard Allen does imply that the duration of a sound contributes to rhythm when he notes that 'The presence of adjacent plosives is mainly perceived by the changed rhythm, caused by the pause made for the unexploded plosive', giving the example 'stop him' / 'we stopped once' / 'we stopped twice'.

Here it might seem that the idea of quantity, and the Elizabethan attempts to write quantitative verse in English, would be relevant. Attridge (1974), however, in his intensive study of those experiments and their background, shows that the writers subordinated the phonic aspect of language to features of spelling and syllable position that belong to the written language. He quotes one Elizabethan scholar's concern for writers who 'knowe no better rules to be directed by in making their Poems and songs than the uncertaine and variable judgement of the eare'. Moreover, drawing on the work of Sidney Allen (1973) and other scholars, he points to the uncertainty which still exists about the nature of 'quantity' even in classical verse; it does not, in spite of traditional belief, denote actual differences in the duration of the 'long' and 'short' syllables. And Attridge notes that it was after facing the shortcomings of their quantitative experiments that Sidney and Spenser reverted to a tradition descended from Chaucer and wrote verse based 'on the phonetic properties of the living language around them'.

It is, of course, possible to elaborate a notation for all those properties, including not only stress pattern but the pattern of syllabic duration and the pattern of pitch change. But this would become intolerably cumbrous in the discussion of verse or prose as literature rather than as language samples.

For his practical teaching purposes Stannard Allen lists a great variety of the common rhythmical groupings of English speech, the groupings in fact which are basic to the reading of literature, poetry or prose. Some are short: come here, what for?, not now. Some are quite long: show him up to his room, walking along the road, tell her not to be late. Many will fit into metrical verse without change, and the longest are so clearly metrical, especially on repetition, that we feel uneasy at having dropped into verse while we speak or while we write prose: I wonder if he'll ask me in advance, we haven't got an envelope to match, we finished it the day before he came; or, even longer, he says that he wants us to take it away, I shouldn't have thought he could get here in time. Allen's list of rhythmical groupings (which incidentally casts great doubt on the uncritically repeated claim that English is a naturally iambic language) is very long, each group with ample examples, and one might even be tempted to imagine that speech is a mosaic of these rhythmical units. But that would be to ignore the other, equally important characteristic of language, its continuity and flow.

Undoubtedly a short unit of speech rhythm often stands by itself, especially with brief questions – whatever for?; brief imperatives – ask him to wait; and exclamations – what a hope! In longer sentences the small units of rhythm can still be distinguished – if necessary isolated while we consider them – but in normal speech or reading they flow into and out of each other, masking their separate identities. The continuity of a clause or a sentence is secured not only by its sense and grammatical form but also by its rhythmical flow.

It is a fairly simple process that produces the flow between one unit of rhythm and the next: between the small units – the rhythmical nuclei – there intervene one or more syllables that can combine rhythmically with either a preceding or a following nucleus. These non-committed syllables create a bridge between groups of sounds that would otherwise stand apart as distinct units. Take an ordinary sentence by Matthew Arnold:

We all of us like to go our own way, and not to be forced out of the atmosphere of commonplace habitual to most of us.

('The literary influence of academies')

Breaking down the first part of the sentence into small rhythmical units and indicating them by exaggerated pauses, we could read it

We all of us   like to go   our own way...

but equally we could divide it

We all of us like   to go our own way...

or

We all of us   like to go our own way...

The ease with which the middle syllables can be distributed to the preceding or to the following unit, or can stand as a unit on their own, prevents any unit standing out sharply in ordinary reading. Similarly we could phrase the latter part of the sentence

and not to be   forced out   of the atmosphere   of commonplace

or

and not to be forced   out of the atmosphere of   commonplace...

We are obliged to take our choice among the phrasings as we read, but the pauses and differentiations of stress are minimal and the chief impression is of continuity.

But near the end of the sentence we seem bound to pause momentarily between 'commonplace' and 'habitual'; although the sense flows continuously, the rhythm does not. The pause is apparently caused by the grammatical break or compression: 'the atmosphere of commonplace [which is] habitual to most of us'. By rephrasing with a different grammatical structure we could preserve the same units of rhythm but make them flow continuously:

...the atmosphere of commonplace which paralyses most of us.

The effect is to bring out the unfortunate jingle of the fourfold 'de-da-de-de': 'the atmosphere of...' Arnold's slight pause after 'commonplace' mitigated that and probably accounts for his not having noticed it.

Consider a flowing sentence by Conrad:

Their bearing, which was simply the bearing of commonplace individuals going about their business in the assurance of perfect safety, was offensive to me like the outrageous flauntings of folly in the face of a danger it is unable to comprehend.

The flow is ensured by the overlapping, through bridging syllables, of different possible units of rhythm:

which was    simply the bearing of    commonplace individuals
which was simply    the bearing of commonplace    individuals
going about    their business    in the assurance of    perfect safety
going about their business    in the assurance    of perfect safety.

The units that overlap are not necessarily units of sense (though they can be) but units of rhythm, and the bridging syllables are often particles which have no greater logical attachment to one nucleus than the other.

Continuously flowing sections of prose (or verse) are generally not long, if only because the sense and grammatical form of sentences and clauses bring divisions that demand some considerable pause. And for various purposes of prose and speech something like a mosaic of disjunct rhythm units does in fact occur. Another brief passage from *The Heart of Darkness* shows Conrad using first a mosaic of disjunct rhythms and then gliding into a longer sentence with the continuous flow of overlapping units:

You should have heard him say, 'My ivory'. Oh yes, I heard him. 'My Intended, my ivory, my station, my river, my –' everything belonged to him. It made me hold my breath in expectation of hearing the wilderness burst into a prodigious peal of laughter that would shake the fixed stars in their places.

Where, in a continuously flowing passage, there are alternative ways of handling the sub-units of rhythm, optional points of pause, the choice has to be made in accordance with the sense and feeling of the passage in relation to its context. We could – but most readers would not – take the last line of Eliot's 'The Hollow Men' as a sort of dactylic gallop –

Not with a    bang but a    whimper.

That might just be defended as emphasizing the bitter nursery-rime quality of the line. But to bring out the contrast between 'bang' and 'whimper', and because of the stress pattern of 'This is the way...', used three times over in the immediately preceding lines, we are virtually bound to phrase it

Not with a bang    but a whimper.

The extent to which we become aware of the rhythms in any continuous flow of language when we speak or listen or read (aloud or silently) depends on our own individual tendency to emphasize or minimize rhythmical patterns and our sense of their importance in a particular passage. It is not always possible to decide from observable features of speech, such as stress and pause in reading aloud, how emphatically or sensitively the reader is responding to the rhythmical pattern. It was long ago shown by H. E. O. James (1926) that when a rhythm has once been suggested by objective differences in the time intervals of a sequence of sounds those differences can be gradually reduced, even in the end obliterated, and the listener will go on experiencing the same rhythmical pattern as he first heard. It seems likely that in the same way somebody reading aloud may be keenly aware of the rhythmical organization of the language but yet not mark it very definitely by pause and stress. Actors and other trained speakers are better than most of us at bringing out clearly the rhythmical patterns they want us to experience. One reason why poets are sometimes ineffective readers of their own verse may be that they are so keenly aware subjectively of their rhythms that they too greatly reduce the objective indicators of pause and stress that we should be glad of.

The conception of rhythm outlined here means that we regard it as closely comparable to shape or form in the visual arts. James Ward (1918) made the point that 'whether simple or complex, the rhythm is an intuited unity as truly as a geometrical figure may be'. It is in fact a Gestalt of successive impressions, closely comparable to the visual configurations whose wholeness and perceptual immediacy the Gestalt psychologists insisted on. The rhythmical units of speech, for instance, are comparable to the shapes that pattern our visual environment: they are like the rectangles and triangles and odd-shaped polygons, the circles and cylinders and ellipses, that go to make up the appearance of our walls and floors, tables and chairs, telephone and typewriter; we can for special purposes attend to these constituent shapes, but in the ordinary way they flow into one another and remain subordinate to the functional whole that we call for instance a table or a chair. It is the interior decorator who has an eye to the visual configurations that make up objects. He notices their height relative to one another, he sees that the pattern in the carpet picks up the design of a mirror frame, or he feels uncomfortable at a visual clutter that for us has the cosiness of a familiar accumulation of usable objects.

So too with speech and prose. We take in mainly the sense, but we can if we wish give special attention to component features of the sound and movement continuum, changes of intonation or tempo for instance, or the pauses and stress patterns which define its units of rhythm. In so far as these units are distinguishable they stand in relation to other units, either immediately adjacent or in the wider context. In the same way a painting consists of visual forms, some subordinate to others, all interrelated and defining themselves against a background of other forms, some standing out in relative isolation while others are hardly noticed as shapes in themselves. And just as a visual form can be given emphasis by repetition, as in a colonnade or regular fenestration on a building, so rhythm units can be made insistent, even obtrusive, by regular metre.

# 2

# Speech and the rhythm of verse

The organized shapes in a painting or a building or a piece of sculpture are selections from the shapes that make up the ordinary visual environment. In the same way even the most highly organized English verse makes use of the stress patterns of ordinary speech; and in recent years critics have more frequently than in the past insisted on the close relation between speech rhythms and verse. Especially when the more mechanical kinds of prosody fail to make sense of a poet's rhythm, a rhythm such as Wyatt's for example, the natural phrasing of speech has been seen to have a function in its own right; if it interrupts a regular metrical pattern but still justifies itself by its rhythmical effect it need not be given fictitious metrical respectability by an elaborate story of 'licences'. When in 1946 I wrote about Wyatt's poetry I took this line without, as far as I knew, much help from scholars, but I find that in the same year Marjorie Daunt (1946) expressed a similar view in a paper called 'Old English verse and English speech rhythms'. In that paper she objects to the assumption underlying earlier criticism 'that a metrical order or regularity, that we can recognize as such, must be produced, lest our ancestors be revealed as devoid of musical sense'. She dissents from C. S. Lewis's paper (1938), 'The fifteenth century heroic line', because, she says, he believes metre to be basic and 'seems to attribute to "metre" an inevitability which I hold to rest on the authenticity of spoken language'. Similarly in 1960 John Holloway, discussing Skelton, wrote 'the result is a loose and exceedingly flexible verse form...which has as its metrical unit not the foot at all, but the self-dependent phrase...It is essentially a metre dominated by the speaking voice, as against a metre which dominates the voice' (p. 19).

This wide acceptance at the present day of some principle other than metre in the ordering of verse goes back at least to the imagists and the writers of free verse earlier this century, but its application by scholars and critics to verse which is largely metrical does imply a relaxation of the more conventional prosodic rigidities. In that way it is a real advance.

At the same time it leaves one question unasked, as well as unanswered. There is undoubtedly a difference between ordinary speech or ordinary prose, each with its succession of rhythmical units, and what we call verse, even forms of verse such as Marjorie Daunt and John Holloway have in mind in which metre is not the main organizing principle. Marjorie Daunt remarks that 'The fact that Shakespeare's verse approximated to natural speech has been accepted for a very long time...'; unfortunately for everyday pleasure, natural speech doesn't approximate very closely to Shakespeare's verse. Marjorie Daunt does touch, but rather lightly, on the problem of what makes verse different. '*Old English verse*' she writes '*is really conditioned prose*, i.e. the spoken language specially arranged with alliteration, but arranged in a way that does no violence to the spoken words.' And again, 'The conclusion drawn here is that in so-called Old English "verse" we are faced with a tidied form of the spoken language, i.e. prose, and that the "pattern" is the pattern of the natural language shapes...' This is entirely convincing as far as it goes but it stops short of saying what, more explicitly, we are to understand by 'conditioned' prose or by 'a tidied form' of the spoken language. Alliteration alone – alliteration without regard to the nature of the line in which it occurs – is not enough to create Old English verse. And much prose, from Sir Thomas Browne to Macaulay, could be called 'conditioned' or 'tidied'. Modern emphasis on the importance of speech rhythms in verse is admirable, but it needs to be supplemented by a clear account of the features of verse that lead us to distinguish it from prose and speech.

The most curious theory of the difference is that the basic characteristic of verse is a succession of identical time intervals between one stressed syllable and the next. A vast amount of scholarly time has been spent in trying to establish this theory of isochronous intervals and – in face of the difficulties that confront it – trying to make compromises that will salvage some part of it.

It seems unlikely that anyone would now want to follow Morris W.

Croll (1929), the American scholar, in his conviction that with patient training, involving a regular tapping of the beat, you can fit all verse into a musical framework, with bars of equal length and an appropriate time signature for different metres. He and William Thomson, whom he was following, understandably wanted to find a more resilient basis for prosody than the notion of a fixed pattern of stressed and unstressed syllables. They recognized that rhythmical units even within metrical verse might combine a main stress with a varying number of lightly stressed syllables. They seem to have felt that this was not a tight enough organization and that there must be some underlying element of uniformity in verse. It was this that they thought they had found by dividing the line into measures of equal duration, each with a main stress, these stresses coming at identical periods of time. 'The equality of time of these periods' says Croll 'is the fundamental fact of rhythm; the rhythm of verse does not arise from equality or similarity in the number of syllables that occupy this time, for the number may vary greatly without disturbing the rhythm, and often silence (or rest) takes the place of one or more syllables.'

Several earlier prosodists had taken a rather similar line, and some later workers have tried to save something of a theory which in its original form they have to reject. Catherine Ing, for example, in *Elizabethan Lyrics* (1951) goes back to the claim of T. S. Omond (1903) that '*isochronous periods* form the units of metre'. She recognizes that this assertion is impossible to sustain. Nevertheless, she argues, if 'uniformity' of time interval is replaced by 'balance' or 'proportion' Omond's theory can be saved and his phrase 'syllabic variety with temporal uniformity' still be used as a description of the rhythmical units of verse. Unfortunately she gives no clear statement of what is to be meant by 'balance' or 'proportion', and a theory which in its original form was definite, though untrue, is replaced by something so vague as to be untestable.

The kind of argument she is reduced to may be illustrated by her account of

> Weep you no more, sad fountains,
> What need you flow so fast?
> Look how the snowy mountains
> Heaven's sun doth gently waste!

'The first two pairs of lines' she writes

certainly have equality, and indeed, it is almost certain that the second and fourth lines will be given silences at the end which make them equal in time to the first and third, though these latter have each one syllable more than the second and fourth. (p. 199)

Dealing with the next five lines,

But my Sun's heavenly eyes   (5)
View not your weeping,   (6)
That now lies sleeping   (7)
Softly, now softly lies   (8)
Sleeping,

she writes

Line five seems to need the same length [as lines one to four which she has persuaded herself into equalizing], lines six and seven are equal to each other though not to the preceding lines, line eight is probably equal to line five, and the final 'sleeping' is a final repeated statement of a part of some of the preceding lines.

And after these dubious, and of course quite untested, claims about the time the lines take to read she concludes rather lamely

Here we have not 'uniformity' between all lines, but certainly 'uniformity' between some, and, I suspect, at least a proportion between these 'uniform' lines and others.

One need hardly labour the point that these vague and cautious claims about the length of lines, even if we accepted them, are extremely remote from the theories of people like Omond and Thomson and Croll that verse depends upon equal periods elapsing between stresses *within* the line.

Convictions about the timing of one's own reading are much too easily supported by self-persuasion to count for much, but even the objective measurement of one reader's timing would have very little relevance, for it would take no account of the variety of legitimate readings, especially of differing lengths of pause within a line and variations of tempo between one line and another. We could, for instance, read the first line slowly, with a fairly long pause after 'more':

Weep you no more,   sad fountains,

and the third line much more rapidly. Variant readings need not be equally attractive – some may strike us as affected – but within wide limits they leave the pattern of the rhythm units and their relation to one another intact. The rhythm units of a fairly regular metre are especially robust and survive big differences of timing between one reader and another.

For a very simple example take Edward Fitzgerald's quatrain about God's responsibility for sin, 'Oh, Thou, who Man of baser Earth didst make'; the last two lines run

> For all the Sin wherewith the Face of Man
> Is blacken'd – Man's forgiveness give – and take!

He indicates the two pauses in the last line by dashes, but their length, especially that of the pause after 'give', can vary widely according to the degree of dramatic emphasis the reader chooses to adopt, but still the shape of the rhythm units and the pattern of their interrelation are preserved. Or consider the lines

> Golden lads and girls all must
> As chimney-sweepers, come to dust.

How long you make the comma-pause at 'chimney-sweepers' depends on how much emphasis you feel should be given to the regretful contrast between golden lads and chimney-sweepers. The metre will not tell you how long to pause and, within wide limits, the rhythms will survive big differences in reading. In face of these very ordinary facts of reading it seems impossible to suppose that equal or even equal-appearing intervals of time are vital to verse. Neither the time occupied in speaking the line nor the proportionate length of one section to the rest of the line is decisive.

Implicitly conceding defeat in her effort to find uniformity of time intervals, Catherine Ing falls back on the idea that 'the pleasure of making rather than finding regularity' explains the satisfaction received from 'highly subtle and variable verse of the madrigal type'. We get, she writes, 'sometimes the satisfaction of regular repetition of small time-divisions within a phrase, sometimes the pleasure of detecting a repetition of complex stress-orders within a simple time-division, sometimes the ease of a steady flow of simple stress-orders in repeated pattern'. Much of this is true, especially when it is phrased in terms of stress patterns, but she still wants to salvage something of the theory of isochronous intervals and she adds

All these satisfactions are, I think, temporal satisfactions. With all of them we feel some need of recognizing a proportion, if not an equality, between divisions of the total duration of stanza or poem. The proportions are not necesarily simple, but that they are present, or at least sought for, seems to be proved by the tendency of all sensitive readers to weigh the syllables and give them sufficient length or a sufficient surrounding of silence to create an impression of careful consideration for the dimension of time in which they exist. (p. 202)

Of course sensitive readers do this, but for many other reasons than an inclination to discover isochronous intervals. With the clear notion of equal duration abandoned in favour of vague, completely undefined 'proportions', and with even these proportions possibly absent from the poem and only to be sought for, it is evident that the search for isochronous intervals as the basis of verse is a will o' the wisp pursuit.

Behind it lies the misconception that rhythm consists in the regular recurrence of events in time. The fact is that the regular repetition of a pattern of sounds or movements may draw our attention to the pattern, or may establish a set that facilitates our perception of the pattern when it recurs, but the pattern itself is independent of its regular recurrence. It is a pattern not because it recurs but because we have made an immediate perceptual whole out of a mere succession of events, and we have done so by perceiving one or more of the events as salient and the others as subordinate.

We still face the question how the rhythms of verse differ from those of the ordinary spoken language from which they are made. On the way to an answer more needs to be said about the mutual relation between metrical verse and the speech rhythms it incorporates.

The differences of rhythm between speech and verse look obvious enough at first sight; but they prove difficult to specify. Metrical verse, with its frequent reminders of the same rhythm unit (or of a pattern of units) offers the simplest contrast to natural speech, and yet, as Marjorie Daunt and John Holloway and many other writers have said, it may include speech rhythms that take precedence over the nominal metre and disrupt the pattern. The place of the natural speaking voice in verse was given a good deal of attention in the second decade of the century. Robert Frost held that 'a man will not easily write better than he speaks when some matter has touched him deeply'. This was sometimes taken as a recommendation that verse should be made up of colloquial phrases that might all be scraps of everyday speech. T. Sturge Moore, a correct and academic poet of the early 1900s, evidently thought Frost was making some such claim, and his misunderstanding was dealt with well and patiently by Edward Thomas in a letter to Gordon Bottomley of 30 June 1915:

Moore was excellent in principle. But in condemning Frost I think still that he had been misled with supposing that Frost wanted poetry to be colloquial. All he insists on is what he believes he finds in all poets – absolute fidelity to the postures which the voice assumes in the most expressive intimate speech. So long as these tones and postures are there he has not the least objection to any vocabulary whatever or any inversion or variation from the customary grammatical forms of talk. In fact I think he would agree that if these tones and postures survive in a complicated and learned or subtle vocabulary and structure the result is likely to be better than if they survive in the easiest form, that is in the very words and structures of common speech, though that is not easy or prose would be better than it is and survive more often...Frost's vocabulary and structure deceive the eye sometimes with thinking it is just statement more or less easily put into easy verse form. But it is not.

(J. Moore, 1939, p. 328)

There are two claims in Thomas's letter. The first can readily be granted: that everyday speech cannot easily be turned into effective verse and that what Frost (and he himself) produced was a subtle and difficult achievement. The other claim is more questionable, that 'a complicated and learned and subtle vocabulary and structure' may be compatible with the tones and postures of voice in intimate speech. The two could seldom have been united in the conventional verse, of indirectly Miltonic ancestry, which would then have been the obvious contrast to Frost. As Leavis (1936) remarked, and compellingly demonstrated, 'the Grand Style barred Milton from essential expressive resources of English that he had once commanded', and Edward Thomas could have had little use for its residue in writers like Sturge Moore. But presumably he saw that writing might differ sharply from everyday contemporary speech (as of course it does in the poetry of earlier centuries) and yet retain essential qualities uniting it with the expressive phrases of spontaneous speech or self-communing. Among these qualities rhythm is pre-eminent.

Hopkins, for instance, has no hesitation in departing widely at times from the ordinary word order of everyday speech but he anchors these departures in speech rhythm, sometimes by enunciating that first:

> Not, I'll not, carrion comfort, Despair, not feast on thee;
> Not untwist – slack they may be – these last strands of man
> In me ór, most weary, cry *I can no more*. I can;
> Can something, hope, wish day come, not choose not to be.
> But ah, but O thou terrible, why wouldst thou rude on me
> Thy wring-world right foot rock?

This is a rare kind of achievement. The force of the simpler speech rhythms is enhanced with repetitions, compressions, and the emphasis given by the alliteration and rimes, internal and line-end. The inversion and the archaic second person singular of the last two lines have a totally different effect, coming after phrases of passionate speech, from the tepid poeticisms of the same devices used simply to fill out the metrical mould. In the opening lines, in fact, the speech rhythms have such strength in their own right, merely as patterns of speaking, that we are hardly aware, if at all, of the metrical scheme.

There are other, totally different ways, in which speech rhythms can be retained in metrical verse. In some sections of *Four Quartets* Eliot has employed abstract discursive prose statements, far from colloquial but doing no violence to speech rhythms; like fairly formal prose they extend by their syntactical structure the amount of utterance that is organized into one continuous whole, but each phrase within it takes the ordinary rhythm of the spoken language. For instance from 'Little Gidding':

> This is the use of memory:
> For liberation – not less of love but expanding
> Of love beyond desire, and so liberation
> From the future as well as the past. Thus, love of a country
> Begins as attachment to our own field of action
> And comes to find that action of little importance
> Though never indifferent.

Verse like this differs from prose by bringing out much more emphatically, largely by the use of the line ending, the rhythmical shape of the component phrases which in prose would pass almost unnoticed in the continuous flow.

Quite often much more colloquial speech rhythms can go direct into metrical verse. 'Nothing so true as what you once let fall', remarks Pope, and it could be a conversational opening as they walked in the garden, until he adds 'Most women have no characters at all'. Sometimes the metre may slightly emphasize stress differences in a phrase that would not sound obtrusively metrical in speech. We could speak of somebody as being so brash that he seems invulnerable in his impudence, but the phrase immediately becomes metrical as the second line of Dryden's couplet on Bishop Burnet:

> Prompt to assayle, and careless of defence,
> Invulnerable in his Impudence.
> (*The Hind and the Panther*, III, 1183-4)

The relations of speech rhythm to metre include two possibilities that might at first seem incompatible: one is that the metrical set established in the lines may determine the choice between two or more available speech rhythms for the words; the other, that the sense of the words can lead us to adopt one out of perhaps several rhythms that can all be reconciled with the metre. But in both cases speech rhythm is basic and inviolable; and a glance at examples of the two possibilities will show that they are not in reality at variance.

The metrical set suggested by a line or established by a previous line is constantly at work to direct our rhythmizing of the words. The statement 'She sat here in her chair' could be spoken quite naturally with two stresses – on 'sat' and 'chair', or perhaps on 'here' and 'chair'. But as a line in Hardy's poem it takes yet another stress pattern because of the metre established in the previous stanza:

> Here is the ancient floor,
> Footworn and hollowed and thin...
>
> Shé sat hére in her cháir...

where the emphasis given to 'She' prepares for the antithesis with 'He' two lines later. As Robinson (1971) puts it in his discussion of metre and rhythm, 'Metre chooses from the rhythmical alternatives the one that creates the metre'.

One of the characteristics that make for variety in Swinburne's verse is the use of phrases that admit of alternative, or even several, accentuations in speech, the metre often establishing an unexpected one. So in a stanza of 'The Triumph of Time' the beat is first set unmistakably –

> Yea, I know this well; were you once sealed mine,
> Mine in the blood's beat, mine in the breath,
> Mixed into me as honey in wine,

– and this then dictates the unusual but perfectly acceptable speech rhythm, with 'and' emphasized,

> Not tíme that sáyeth ánd gáinsáyeth,
> Not all strong things had severed us then.

In *Macbeth* we probably adopt the stress pattern

> I have lív'd lóng enóugh: my way of life
> Is fall'n into the sere, the yellow leafe...

but in 'Hymn to Proserpine' the same phrase has to run

> Í have líved long enóugh, having seen one thing, that love hath an end;
> Goddess and maiden and queen, be near me now and befriend.

In prose again we should probably read 'Which háth in it áll sóunds...' but in 'Hertha' the pattern established for the last line of each stanza dictates the stress

> Which hath ín it áll sóunds and áll sécrets of ínfinite lánds and of séas.

Sometimes, too, Swinburne's metre will vary the stress on a repeated word. In prose we might read 'Had you chósen, had you strétched hánd, had you séen góod...' but in 'The Triumph of Time' the metre emphasizes 'you' at three points and leaves it unstressed at one:

> But yóu, had you chósen, had yóu strétched hánd,
> Had yóu seen góod such a thíng were dóne...

And we need not go to Swinburne for the sort of metre that determines the choice of speech rhythm. Taken out of context Donne's phrase 'Hee, who could do no iniquity' would be given a prose rhythm quite different in stress and phrasing from what it receives in 'Holy Sonnet xi':

> For Í have sínn'd and sínn'd, and only hée,
> Who cóuld dó   nó iníquity   hath dýed.

In all these instances the metrical emphases never replace or distort a speech rhythm but select one out of several that natural speech could adopt on different occasions. Browning very obviously uses metre in this way. Some of his characteristic effects are gained by a trick of leaving the metrical stress almost hidden among adjacent syllables that might have received equal or greater stress in ordinary speech. The result is sometimes to avoid metrical stress on a word to which the sense gives emphasis. Robinson (1971) overlooks this device and concludes, mistakenly I think, that some lines in 'The Lost Leader' are 'unintentionally unmetrical'. Quoting five lines, he says that 'There is no way of making the metre we find in the first two lines co-operate with the language in the third and following lines; the tension – the attempt to find a metrical way of reading – is still un-resolved as the words are spoken' (p. 61). The difficulty arises from the fact that such phrases as 'one wrong more to man', 'one task more declined', are most readily spoken with a sense emphasis on 'more', but although 'more' occurs repeatedly in the five lines as a focus of the sense, Browning never gives it metrical stress:

> Stíll bidding cróuch whom the rést bade aspíre:
> Blót out his náme, then, – recórd one lost sóul more,
> One tásk more declíned, one more fóotpath untród,
> One more tríumph for dévils, and sórrow for ángels,
> One wróng more to mán, one more ínsult to Gód!

(I have indicated the speech stresses that maintain the metre.) The phrase 'record one lost soul more' illustrates Browning's knack of accompanying the stresses with adjacent syllables which are un-stressed but still sense-emphasized, a device that contributes to his air of highly compressed meaning. It is from among several possible sense-emphases that the reader has to seek the stress which also maintains the four-beat shape of each line. Even in such lines from Browning the metre is not violating speech rhythms; those it estab-lishes are unexpected but still possible in emphatic speech.

The second, contrasting possibility is that quite different rhythms, in the sense of patterns of pause and stress (accompanied by differ-ences of intonation), might be adopted in the same line of a metrical poem, the choice among them being determined not by the metre but by our reading of the sense. The great flexibility of the iambic pentameter in English verse especially offers this choice. Think for instance of the diverse but metrically acceptable readings of Pope's line, 'Most women have no characters at all'. It could be taken as contrasting women with men: 'Most *women* have...' Or it could be leading to the statement that one woman, in contrast to the majority, does have a character: '*Most* women have...' But in fact the lines that follow imply that 'characters' here means clear and consistent distinguishing marks:

> Matter too soft a lasting mark to bear,
> And best distinguished by black, brown, or fair.

How many pictures of one nymph we view,
All how unlike each other, all how true!

And for this context the phrasing and emphases and intonation would be different:

Móst women *háve*   no *cháracters*   at áll.

There could be yet other minor diversities of reading, all acceptable within the metrical poem. The rhythm we adopt is not dictated by the metre but chosen from several possible speech rhythms according to the sense.

The older students of verse were not always willing to concede this. William Thomson (1923) reproduces the phrasing offered by an early twentieth century actor, Lewis Waller, in giving the speech of Henry V before Harfleur. Thomson says that 'the actor, following the usual stage tradition, makes no attempt at rhythmization to bring out verse-structure. He frankly speaks the lines as prose, and accordingly only those that, as such, are furnished with five accents make any pretension to movement as verse'. And Thomson gives his own alternative readings that preserve what he regards as the verse structure. For instance, Waller said 'Hóld hárd the bréath, and bénd up évery spírit' – but that gives six accents to the line, so Thomson reads 'Hold hárd the bréath, and bénd up évery spírit'. Again, Waller said 'Stíffen the sínews, súmmon up the blóod' – only four accents, so Thomson offers 'Stíffen the sínews, súmmon úp the blóod'. It seems in the highest degree unlikely that Shakespeare, working all his life in the theatre, expected players to sacrifice effective speech rhythms to a metrical scheme.

There happens also to be a record of subtler differences in the way nineteenth century actors spoke lines of Shakespeare. George Darley, the critic and minor poet, wrote on 24 October 1822 to Marianne Neail

You have heard I dare say of the three characteristic readings of that sentiment in *Hamlet* –

He was a man, Horatio, take him for all in all,
I neer shall look upon his like again.

(This is Kemble's & in my opinion the natural sense of the lines.)

He was a *man*, Horatio: – take him for all in all,
I neer shall look upon his like again.

(This is Kean's & has his peculiar characteristic of catching at energetical *points*.)

He was a man, Horatio, take him for all in all: –
I neer shall look upon his like again.

(This is said to be Young's, & I confess myself wholly unable to appreciate its judiciousness. It conveys nothing but that Hamlet's father was a rational two-legged animal, called a man, of which no one had expressed any doubt. It has not Kean's idea of the unlimited perfection of manhood, nor Kemble's (or rather Shakespeare's idea of manhood as perfect as human frailty would allow.)

(Abbott, 1967, p. 23)

These differences of emphasis and pause are all compatible with the preservation of the verse line; they are altogether different from the mangling of Shakespeare by many actors in the third quarter of the twentieth century who turned the verse into prose by throw-away mutterings or disrupted the line by breaking off in the middle for prolonged emotional contortions – those attempts at creativeness in delivery went beyond the great latitude of rhythm that the Shakespearian line permits without being destroyed as a line.

The poet's own concern to establish the primacy of a particular speech rhythm appears plainly in those awkward instances where the metre could have suggested an unwanted rhythm and he finds himself infelicitously reduced to italicizing (or, in Hopkins, using stress marks). Thus in 'The Aeolian Harp' Coleridge speaks of the scents

Snatch'd from yon bean-field! and the world *so* hushed!

where neither the metre nor the sense would have suggested un-equivocally the rhythm 'and the wórld só húshed'. Italicizing is a clumsy device (or, as in some of Byron, one that asserts the casual, comic style of versification), but there are many instances where, without it, the rhythm the poet had in mind is uncertain and the reader makes his own choice. (Even in music, with a much more closely controlling notation, the performer must to some extent choose his own rhythmical phrasing.) Certainly a metrical set as loose and accommodating as the so-called iambic in English will seldom be decisive in the choice between alternative possibilities of speech rhythm.

The rhythms of natural speech are an intrinsic part of the language, often reflecting (with the associated intonation) the sense in which a phrase with more than one possible meaning has been taken. Verse, especially metrical verse, can indicate which among possible rhythms is intended, but it must always be a rhythm possible in natural speech. This rhythmical demand holds even if the manner of reading is not in other ways natural – is, for instance, declamatory or incantatory; still the rhythmical pattern is inviolable. And when the only available speech rhythms depart from the pattern suggested by the strict simplicity of a regular metre it is the simple regularity that has to be sacrificed.

# 3

# Metrical set and
# rhythmical variation

When a speech rhythm deviates from the metre of a poem in an agreeable way the conventional prosodists have justified the devia-tion as a 'licence', that being a gesture of verbal magic through which a non-metrical phrase is deemed to be metrical. As far as I can see, it is simply a description post factum of any rhythmical deviation from metre that poets have used with undeniable success. What the more modern prosodists maintain is not always clear. Most of them have retreated from such a position as Thomson's when he seeks ways of finding the right number of accents for the line even if he has to override natural phrasing and emphasis. Seymour Chatman (1964) recognizes that the stress pattern of a line of metrical verse is not necessarily fixed but may vary with different readings (which need not be of equal merit). This admission brings in question the reality of the so-called metre. But Chatman resorts to the suggestion that 'the meter of any poem is best described as the matrix of all mean-ingful scansions' (p. 104), a statement that sounds more impressive than the fact that it tries to cope with.

This fact is that a line occurring in a mainly metrical poem can often be read with several different rhythmical groupings, and the 'metre' in the old sense is not decisive in our choice among them. To call the range of choices a metrical matrix suggests that there is still some controlling principle at work other than simple speech rhythms. Where there really is, where the influence of previous metrical lines helps to determine which of the possible speech rhythms we actually adopt, then there is a controlling metrical pattern in the old sense; otherwise no principle beyond meaning and acceptable rhythms of speech is involved. But the discussion of this point becomes a matter of mysterious abstractions. Chatman's footnote (p. 105) refers to

W. K. Wimsatt and M. Beardsley, 'The concept of meter: An exercise in abstraction', *PMLA*, LXXIV (1959), who discuss 'whether there is one meter necessarily common to all acceptable performances of a poem'; and to Rulon Wells, *Style in Language*, who 'seems to agree that all the different possible interpretations of a line need not have the same meter, although they may'. It looks as if this last ditch prosody is making strenuous verbal attempts to save the name of metre while relinquishing virtually all the older claims for it as a framework guiding the writer and the reader.

Chatman sums up his view in saying that rhythm is a percept, accessible to any human being with ears, but metre is a concept. 'It is the mind, not the senses, which performs the task of reducing disparate linguistic phenomena to simple distinctions, learning to measure and equate things which are very different indeed in their absolute physical nature' (p. 105). This clearly implies that metre will not directly affect the way you read or hear a line; there will only be the additional knowledge that the rhythms can be made to square with some very abstract scheme, a scheme which can only be deduced, not perceived, and which has no influence on reading.

The work of Halle and Keyser (1971) similarly develops, and in an especially puzzling way, the view that metre is an abstraction. Concentrating on the iambic pentameter, they point out that the listing of allowable deviations (or licences), by orthodox English prosodists such as Bridges, besides being doubtfully complete also gives far too much latitude if taken literally, since by combining enough 'allowable deviations' within one line you can claim as an iambic pentameter a sequence of words that no one would feel to be an iambic line at all. As their example of a non-iambic 'line' they ingeniously take

Ode to the West Wind by Percy Bysshe Shelley

and show that by invoking a number of recognized licences you could claim that this is, after all, an iambic pentameter. That nonsense result, they point out, comes about because the ordinary account of allowable deviations confines itself to what may happen within any one 'foot' and implies that 'deviations in one foot are independent of deviations in adjoining feet' (p. 166).

In their own system they make a valuable advance by discarding the concept of the foot altogether; they take the iambic pentameter to consist not of five feet but of nine to twelve syllables, the perfectly regular, or simplest, line being of ten syllables with alternate weak and strong stresses. They then devise with great resourcefulness a number of formulations to describe such deviations from this simplest pattern as still leave the line acceptable in iambic pentameter verse, simple or increasingly complex. And negatively, but crucially, they show that such a sequence of words as

Ode to the West Wind by Percy Bysshe Shelley

is excluded. Their formulations have been disputed by some scholars and may need modifications and elaborations to do all that they claim.

Suppose, however, that the system could be made watertight and complete, the question is what would have been achieved. It comes oddly to find them saying at the end of their account that this metrical analysis has no bearing on the way the lines are read. They have for example given their analysis of a line by Donne:

Yet déarly I lóve you and would be lóvĕd fáin

where for their metrical justification of the line the third and fourth syllables, 'ly I', have to be counted as occupying one weak position, and the sixth and seventh, 'you and', similarly occupy one weak position. Their handling of the syllables would seem to make the line almost equivalent rhythmically to

Yet déar I lóve and would be lóvĕd fáin.

But, they say, 'The assignment of syllables to position is, of course, strictly metrical. It does not imply that the syllables assigned to a single position should be slurred or elided when the verse is recited.' Their rules 'are not instructions for poetry recitation. They are, rather, abstract principles of verse construction whose effect on the sound of the recited verse is indirect' (pp. 171–2). This seems to mean that it would be legitimate to read Donne's line

Yet déarly Í lóve yóu and would be lóvĕd fáin...

while at the same time as we articulate and hear it in this way we should reflect intellectually that it could be thought of in another way that would bring it within the rules of the iambic pentameter. Whether we could reach this intellectual recognition without also imagining the sound or speech movements of the line read in the iambic pattern they don't say.

The attempt to dissociate prosodic analysis from the sound and movement of reading is especially curious in this work of Halle and Keyser in view of the foundation on which they rest their whole treatment of the subject. For they take as their datum the subjective impression, which they claim all readers will share, that certain lines are not in iambic metre, others are in simple iambic, and others in more complex iambic. They are explicit that this is their basic fact, and they offer no other criterion. This criterion necessarily depends on the actual sound or articulation of the words; they then assert that their rules for describing which stress patterns are consistent with iambic pentameter so assessed are quite independent of the way the words sound. The conclusion contradicts the initial assumption. I believe this contradiction lurks in any prosodic scheme that tries to free itself from the actual experience of sound and speech movement in which metre originates.

In the last chapter of his book Chatman turns to the literary function of metre, saying that 'one studies meter not only, or even primarily, as an interesting physical and psychological phenomenon, but to discover more about poetry'. Once he undertakes this part of the problem he leaves aside his conception of metre as an abstraction and follows conventional lines, examining the literary effectiveness of perfectly perceptible features of rhythm, tempo and intonation in metrical verse. For these purposes of enjoyment and critical understanding he is in accord with the much more usual – but still mistaken – view that the nominal metrical scheme does in some way affect our pronunciation of the syllable sequences that depart from it, and not simply by the elisions, slurrings or hurryings that ordinary speech can include. The metrical scheme, according to this view, violates in some degree the natural way of rhythmizing the language. Take for instance Blake's line

O rádiant mórning, salúte the sún...

a rhythmical exclamation. It seems impossible to believe with Alicia Ostriker (1965) that its effectiveness is enhanced by the fact that 'one's reading adjusts slightly to what the metrical beat was expected to be:

Ŏ rádĭánt mŏrníng, sălúte thĕ sún.

The net effect includes a kind of sustaining of -ing, which is assisted by the ensuing pause, and which helps to produce the lyric's effect of eager pleading' (p. 37). I should argue that the sense and the comma pause are enough to sustain -ing as much as need be, and that any real departure from the normal pronunciation of 'morning' is an unjustified distortion of the English language. John Thompson (1961) similarly tries to maintain a distinction between the metrical pattern and 'how the line might be spoken'; he scans (using ˢ for stressed and ᵒ for unstressed) Milton's line

       ᵒ     ˢ      ᵒ      ˢ      ᵒ  ˢ      ᵒ ˢ      ᵒ    ˢ
With head, / hands, wings, / or feet / pursues / his way.

And he adds

The reading, in whatever voice the reader uses for Milton, would probably show some compromise between the metrical pattern and the phrase pattern the ordinary uses of speech would suggest. (p. 8)

If it did it would be doing violence to English, and needlessly.

Whether the metrical scheme or the sense of the words determines our choice between alternative rhythms in verse, the one chosen must be acceptable in ordinary speech; the established rhythm of the spoken language is basic and inviolable. (Many song settings of course distort it at will, but they claim no relation to speech.) In the reading by William Thomson, quoted earlier, of the speech before Harfleur, it happens that an insistence on the simple metrical stressing produces a not impossible speech rhythm, though one ignoring the emphases that best reinforce the sense. But what of other lines of verse where a much more definite collision occurs between the nominal metre and inescapable speech rhythm? Tennyson's 'Ulysses' has the lines about Ulysses' conventional son:

> Most blameless is he, centred in the sphere
> Of common duties, decent not to fail
> In offices of tenderness, and pay
> Meet adoration to my household gods,
> When I am gone.    He works his work, I mine.

It is this last sentence, 'Hé works hís work, Í míne' (with 'He' and 'his' stressed, but 'works' and 'work' kept prominent by the slight pause that follows them), which causes trouble. Thomson 'gives up this line as altogether unmetrical', according to J. C. Pope (1942).

But J. C. Pope himself struggles on. He accentuates the troublesome sentence

> Hè wórks hìs wórk, Ì míne,

using secondary accents as well as primary, and, he says, 'allowing the secondary accents to be virtually as strong as the primary, but much inferior to what they would normally be, and retaining a slightly elevated pitch on *He*, *his*, and *I*' (p. 13, footnote). Such a reading is so contorted that, if we had to choose between them, Thomson's acceptance of the speech rhythms and abandonment of the metre would be preferable. But it takes prosodists to discover a difficulty here; the natural speech phrasing comes as a perfectly acceptable change of rhythm to end what is in effect a verse paragraph. As J. A. Symonds urged readers, 'Attend strictly to the sense and the pauses: the lines will then be perfectly melodious; but if you attempt to scan the lines on any preconceived metrical system, you will violate the sense and vitiate the music' (quoted by Mayor (1901)).

That half line from 'Ulysses' is only an unusually clear instance of what is continually happening in metrical verse. A little further on in the poem are two lines in which speech rhythms do coincide with the nominal metre:

> Some wórk of nóble nóte, may yét be dóne,
> Not únbecóming mén that stróve with Góds.

But then come rhythms that depart widely and effectively from the regular iambic beat:

> The líghts begin to twínkle from the rócks:
> The lóng dáy wánes: the slów móon clímbs: the déep
> Móans róund with mány vóices.　Cóme, my fríends...

You could, of course, but quite artificially, approach regular metre in these lines by pretending that some of the heavy stresses are light and some of the light stresses heavy:

> The líghts begín to twínkle fróm the rócks:
> The lóng day wánes: the slów moon clímbs: the déep...

This would be such a travesty of the movement of the lines that presumably no prosodist would ever have read it like that (though it is often uncertain what prosodists have intended).

At first sight a more plausible case is offered by Catherine Ing when she discusses (p. 144) Michael Drayton's 'Agincourt', claiming that departures from ordinary speech stress are dictated by the metre and justified by the suggestion of the emphatic 'heavy marching tread' constantly repeated. The stress on the first syllable of each line – Fair stood the wind for France – must be preserved, she argues, even though 'such words as "and" must at times take stress nearly as heavy as that on the first syllable of "marcheth"' –

> And taking many a fort,
> Furnished in warlike sort,
> Marcheth towards Agincourt
>   In happy hour;
>
> Skirmishing day by day
> With those that stopped his way,
> Where the French general lay
>   With all his power.

Yet even here there is doubt. We can certainly, if we wish, give stress to 'And' in 'And taking many a fort', but this is by no means an impossible speech emphasis when you want to secure a cumulative effect: the metre guides us in choosing between two possible speech rhythms. In the next stanza, however, nothing is gained by reading '*With* those that stopped his way'; nor in the first stanza by adopting the rhythm 'Whén we our sáils advánce'. Where, as here, metre conflicts with natural speech, the speech rhythm prevails, with the gain of creating variety within the marching thud of the general scheme.

The notion that our reading should ever be some kind of 'compromise' between metre and natural speech is indefensible. Different readings may legitimately give minor variations of pause and stress in the line

> Thrée   Ápril pérfumes in   thrée   hót   Júnes   búrned

but any 'compromise' with

> Three Á / pril pér / fumes ín / three hót / Junes búrned

would be ruinous. Or take an example from theatre verse. Before the entrance of Banquo's ghost Macbeth has the lines

> I drink to th' general joy o' th' whole table,
> And to our dear friend Banquo, whom we miss;
> Would he were here!

In the second line, to convey the insincere emphasis, there must be a firm stress on 'And' and the nominal metrical stress on 'to' must be ignored; any adjustment or compromise between the two would blunt the point. In the third line the phrase would probably be patterned 'Wóuld he were hére!' (repeating the pattern 'Ánd to our déar'), but it could also be taken 'Would hé were hére!', the nominal iambic beat being followed. Whichever the actor chose he would have to relinquish the other, not compromise. He could, of course, make a spondee, with a stress on both 'Would' and 'he', but this is simply a third possibility of speech rhythm, to be chosen for its sense, not dictated by the metrical framework although readily accommodated within it.

Another instance occurs in *The Winter's Tale*, where Paulina is contrite for her scourging tongue which has distressed Leontes:

> ...do not receive affliction
> At my petition; I beseech you, rather
> Let me be punish'd, that have minded you
> Of what you should forget...

If we followed the nominal metre in the third line we should put the stress on 'me': 'Let mé be púnished...', as if there were someone else who might be. It is just conceivable that Leontes' affliction is being thought of as a punishment and that she asks to be punished instead of him. But equally good and perhaps preferable sense is made by putting the emphasis on 'punish'd: 'Lét me be *púnish'd*...' Whichever sense is taken the consequent speech rhythm must be clearly adopted and the alternative discarded. No 'compromise' with the metre will do.

Occasionally, if the sense of a line is not immediately obvious, the simple metre will suggest a misreading, as it does in the *Macbeth* lines

> No, this my hand will rather
> The multitudinous seas incarnadine,
> Making the green one red.

The first three Folios printed 'Greene one, Red'; and though the comma after 'one' may have been, as it is said to have been at times, a sign that 'one' should be emphasized, it could easily be taken as a confirmation of the misreading. Some later editors tried other forms of punctuation to convey the meaning:

> the green, One red (Johnson); the green – one red (Steevens).

All such efforts aim to establish the rhythm

> Máking the gréen    óne réd.

Once the sense is clear we adopt the appropriate rhythm, over-riding the nominal metre.

*Troilus and Cressida* provides a more striking instance, where the stress suggested by the metre contributed to the notorious misreading

> One tóuch of nature makes the whole world kin...

It is only the meaning of the line in its context that necessitates deviation from the simple iambic pattern and putting the stress on 'One' (with a different pattern of pitch as well):

> *Óne* touch of nature makes the whole world kin,
> That all with one consent praise new-born gawds,
> Though they are made and moulded of things past.

Here again, as in innumerable passages of verse, the sense, with the speech rhythms it dictates, must take precedence of any mechanical form of the nominal metre, and must do so decisively, without compromise.

The idea that metre may warrant an 'adjusted' – as I would say, a distorted – speech rhythm is sometimes lightheartedly combined with a belief in the importance of a counterpointing between an expected metrical pattern and the deviation that actually comes. In reality the two views are mutually incompatible – if we 'adjust' our speech rhythm we iron out the deviation – and the latter view, of counterpointing, is undoubtedly the more challenging and the more difficult to assess. The idea is that our expectation of the regular beat makes us experience some 'tension' between that and what we actually meet. ('Tension' is here a metaphor; what it may more literally refer to is very obscure.) In musical counterpoint, as far as I understand, the contrasting melodies are both present and can be really heard by the skilled listener. The process supposed to occur in verse must be more complex, since one of the patterns is only imagined. Before going on (in the following chapter) to examine this theory it is necessary to look more closely at the nature of the metrical pattern and the expectations against which the actual rhythms are supposed to be counterpointed.

To give the view a fair run it is best to discard the word 'expectation'. It might imply some conscious anticipation, and as far as we do anticipate anything about the rhythm of good verse we anticipate variety; it is only in doggerel that we expect complete regularity. However, we can replace 'expectation' with the more general term 'set'. We can suppose that a metrical pattern, especially an emphatic or repeated pattern, may establish a readiness to rhythmize subsequent lines in the same pattern, and this can be some entirely non-conscious readiness of a neuromuscular kind. We may well not become aware of it unless we deliberately analyse the metrical scheme. It is this kind of set which, according to the counterpoint theory, would be in tension with the rhythm actually offered. So, for instance, we could say that in reading eighteenth century verse we have a strong 'set' for the iambic pentameter couplet, although after some acquaintance we have the 'expectation' that it will be varied with an occasional Alexandrine.

To say just what features of a passage of verse establish the metrical set is often surprisingly difficult. 'The repetition of a stress pattern' is the obvious answer; but it turns out that the repetition need not be at all exact or extensive. Swinburne's verse illustrates the point. In the line previously quoted from 'The Triumph of Time' we know from the swing of the preceding lines that 'you' has to be stressed, unstressed and stressed on its three occurrences:

> But yóu,   had you chósen,   had yóu strétched hánd...

But what are the features of the earlier lines that constrain us to give it that pattern? They are not to be specified in terms of anapaests and iambs in any fixed order; the variation is much too great for that. To speak of a mixed iambic-anapaestic metre may specify the ingredients of the mixture but not their proportions nor the order in which they come. Of course, the mould of the poem is, as a matter of immediate perception, unquestionably different from that of nominally iambic verse. Yet before accepting any such easy labelling as explanatory we have to notice that even a firmly defined framework of metre allows such wide latitude (in its so-called licences) that the rhythm of one and the same line can sometimes be accommodated to sharply different metrical sets. A pastiche will illustrate the point:

> Lost sight of, hidden away out of sight,
> Who can foretell for what high cause
> We had grown as gods, as the gods above,
> Ere with their glancing wheels they drive
> In the clamour and rumour of life to be.

Although nonsense, the passage provides, metrically, a sequence of not incompatible lines. But they come, alternately, from Swinburne's 'The Triumph of Time' and Marvell's 'The Picture of little T. C. in a Prospect of Flowers', poems entirely different in metre.

Even pairs of lines taken alternately from the one poem and the other will run together without sharp dislocations, though with less ease than single lines alternating:

> I wish we were dead together today,
> Lost sight of, hidden away out of sight,
> Who can foretell for what high cause
> This darling of the Gods was born!

But with three successive lines from each poem the difference of metrical framework becomes inescapable:

> I wish we were dead together today,
> Lost sight of, hidden away out of sight,
> Clasped and clothed in the cloven clay,
> Who can foretell for what high cause
> This darling of the Gods was born!
> Yet this is she whose chaster laws...

The conventional labelling of the metres of such poems as these is a fiction demanding so many 'licences' that it fails to show what in reality has created the perceived difference between the two rhythmical contexts.

Inspection shows that the crucial difference is the occurrence at least once in each of the Swinburne lines of the rhythm dá-de-de-dá, the stress version of the choriamb. In the three successive lines from Marvell it occurs only once:

> Whó can foretéll...

but in those by Swinburne four times, and at least once in every line:

> I wísh we were déad...
> togéther todáy...
> awáy out of síght...
> clóthed in the clóven...

It is the frequent occurrence of this pattern, though not at any fixed point in the line, that marks the three Swinburne lines as having a different rhythmical swing from that of the three Marvell lines. And for my pastiche the selection of a couple of Marvell lines that include this rhythmical unit makes them metrically assimilable to the Swinburne lines. The conclusion must be that to speak of an English poem as being in some particular metre often suggests constraints which are really not there (as the tale of 'licences' testifies) and at the same time fails to specify the essential features of the rhythmical framework which do establish a set and facilitate certain patterns of rhythmization – and exclude others – as we continue reading.

In the subtler verse forms (such as the late Shakespearian line discussed in Chapter 4) the effective framework is very difficult to identify. Even in such a definite and strongly marked verse form as Swinburne's it is not easy. In the main, in his characteristic verse, you find yourself prepared for a line of four stresses with at least one unstressed syllable between successive stresses, and always at some point in the line two unstressed syllables between them;

> This woven raiment of nights and days,
> Were it once cast off and unwound from me,
> Naked and glad would I walk in thy ways...

But the set so established is flexible enough to accept occasional lines that have five stresses, three coming together instead of being separated by an unstressed syllable:

> As the flów of the fúll séa rísen to flóod...
> Though we séek lífe thróugh, we shall súrely fínd...

Very rarely an iambic line can be carried without disrupting the set, as, from 'Atalanta in Calydon',

> Is half assuaged for Itylus.

But few lines of that pattern could occur without breaking Swinburne's metrical mould, with the loss of his characteristic swinging movement. The occurrence somewhere in each line of two unstressed syllables between stresses is in fact a major means of establishing the set. Its striking importance can be seen by eliminating the crucial extra syllable:

> The dream that smote with keener dart
> Than shafts of love or spears of death,

simple iambic lines, to which Swinburne's addition of one syllable in each gives his familiar swing:

> The dream that smote with a keener dart
> Than shafts of love or arrows of death.

The inclusion of this choriambic unit at least once in each line decisively distinguishes Swinburne's metrical framework in poems like 'The Triumph of Time' from the iambic form of the four-stress line such as Marvell used.

The slightness of the change needed to make a line assimilable first to one rhythmical context and then to another so different is remarkable. The question *why* some particular small change of pattern makes a group of syllables sufficiently like another to be accepted into the same rhythmical set is probably unanswerable, perhaps a nonsense question. There is an analogy in the perception of visual shapes. If we have a series of roughly drawn circles and another of roughly drawn squares, the two series gradually getting more like each other, there will come a point where one figure, an approximate circle with a hint of four corners, could be assimilated to either series; a quite small alteration in it would make it too circular for the squares or too square for the circles. We can't say 'why'. All we can do – and it is to the corresponding task that Halle and Keyser have applied intensive effort – is to devise a general description of the stimulus conditions in which, say, squareness ceases to be perceived; in their case the point at which we can no longer assimilate a line of verse to a series of very variable 'iambic pentameters'.

When a poem has no obtrusively regular metre such as the older scansion into feet could specify with any plausibility, we judge whether some metrical set has nevertheless been established by noting whether our choice among different possible speech rhythms for a phrase is controlled by rhythmical features of previous lines; and more subjectively we experience a 'rightness' as the successive phrases fit into the rhythmical set prepared for them. It is much easier to be aware of the effects of a metrical set than to say precisely what features of the lines provide the constraints which guide us. For most purposes there is no need to identify and label those constraints. From the literary standpoint the more important question about a metrical set is what effect it has, if any, on the complex of satisfactions we find in the poem. And this includes the question whether its effect depends on the reader's experience of counter-pointing between what it prepares him for and what he actually meets.

# 4

# Effects of deviation from metre

When a metrical set has been created in a poem the literary questions arise whether a departure from its simplest outline takes the form of a rhythm acceptable in that context rather than a breakdown, whether the rhythm has any meaningful relation to the sense and feeling, and whether the fact that it is a deviation has any definable significance in the poem. These are questions to be explored, and the findings may not be the same in different poems. It is difficult to accept the easy sweep of one of I. A. Richards' early remarks in *Principles of Literary Criticism* where, after saying that rhythm and metre depend on repetition and expectancy, he goes on

Equally where what is expected recurs and where it fails, all rhythmical and metrical effects spring from anticipation. (p. 134)

'All rhythmical and metrical effects' – this is an immense claim and I believe impossible to sustain. Recalling some of the extensive and subtle effects attributed to rhythm by critics I mentioned earlier we can reasonably ask *how* expectation or anticipation operates to produce them. Those who give such weight to expectancy ought to show in some detail what it may be supposed to do and how it works.

Occasionally this is possible. Robert Frost's 'The Pasture' offers a clear example of a poem where rhythmical variation within a metrical set undoubtedly creates a specifiable effect. In its two stanzas the speaker announces small farm tasks he is setting out to do, necessary tasks but described with an undertone of apology because he is obviously a poet anticipating contemplative pleasure as well as a farmer setting off to do a chore:

> I'm going out to clean the pasture spring;
> I'll only stop to rake the leaves away
> (And wait to watch the water clear, I may)...

The poem has only two four-line stanzas, and the first three lines of each stick closely to the five-stress iambic pattern, so closely that the sharply different rhythm of the fourth line brings a slight jolt as the set is disturbed:

> I shan't be gone long. – You come too.

That fourth line helps to establish the fact that the poem is implicitly a dramatic dialogue. Half apologizing to his companion at leaving her for what he knows will be largely a quiet pleasure, he then switches to inviting her to abandon her occupations and condone his enjoyment of stolen time by joining him. The last line introduces a little dramatic twist; the interruption of regular metrical repetition reinforces a break in the psychological continuity of what is said. 'I shan't be gone long' most naturally implies a parting, but there comes a slight social dislocation as the apparent leave-taking is suddenly replaced by an invitation to companionship. The pause between two stressed syllables in succession emphasizes this psychological switch, with the invitation coming as an afterthought: 'I shan't be gone lóng. – Yóu come too.'

The effect would be lost if either the rhythmical break or the psychological switch were sacrificed. We can easily try it. Abandoning the dramatic shift but keeping the rhythm he could have said

> I shan't be gone long. – Soon be home

– just an ordinary leave-taking. Keeping the switch to proposed companionship but relinquishing the change of rhythm, he could have said

> I shan't be very long. – Will you come too?

which makes the invitation more casual, less of an urged temptation.

The pattern that Frost set out in the first stanza is repeated exactly in the second, with the effect of a ritual game. Again the first three lines have the five strong stresses alternating regularly with weak stresses to establish a set very firmly, and again the fourth line disrupts it:

> I shan't be gone long. – You come too.

And here the total effect of the poem does demonstrably depend on the carefully contrived disturbance of a metrical set. (Notice too that the effectiveness of the poem survives long acquaintance, even when we know exactly what to 'expect' – a fact not to be reconciled with the idea that the effect depends on any conscious expectation.)

Faced with such a definite instance we have a choice between two lines of argument. We might claim that a process of creating and partially disrupting a metrical set, with expressive effect that can occasionally be shown to occur in very clear form, is probably at work with less easily identified effects all through verse. Alternatively we might argue that if at particular points a variant line can be shown so clearly to have a specifiable effect we should be chary of claiming similar effects in general terms without being able to indicate what they are. To say that metrical variations, through the mere fact of being variations, are always producing slight – but unspecifiable – expressive effects is one of those completely untestable and unprofitable assertions that leave us where we were.

I believe that some, but few, metrical deviations do produce an expressive effect simply by altering a previous set, but always through their relation to the sense and feeling; and when they do, it should be possible to say at least in broad outline what is being achieved by the disturbance. Commonly the deviation will do its work through enhancing, by the emphasis of contrast, an expressive effect that the unexpected rhythm would have had in its own right, standing by itself. For example, we could say in prose that this was the position of the door, now long forgotten, where the dead feet walked in. The last phrase, 'where the dead feet walked in', seems even in prose to have a heavy movement fitting the sombreness of the idea, a quality enhanced when the words create a rhythmical variation in Hardy's poem:

> Here is the ancient floor,
> Footworn and hollowed and thin,
> Here was the former door
> Where the dead feet walked in.

Or think again of Tennyson's rhythms,

> The long day wanes: the slow moon climbs...

where he may have been influenced by Antony's words

> ...the long day's task is done.

The succession of prolonged monosyllables makes brisk utterance almost impossible (and Tennyson slightly labours the point by introducing the actual word 'slow'), and the rhythm has much of its effect without the help of a metrical context. The fact that it disturbs the mainly iambic beat of the poem and contrasts still more sharply with the immediately preceding line

The líghts   begin to twínkle   from the shóre

does enhance its effect, but what is enhanced is an expressive value that the rhythm possesses in its own right as a segment of speech and not by virtue of being a deviation from the regular metre. A rhythm poor in itself, ineffective or inappropriate, will gain nothing from being a form of counterpoint. When an effective rhythm is enhanced in expressive value by deviating from the metre, this can be adequately described as a contrast effect. Such effects, when they do occur, can be pointed out. There is no good reason to suppose that they are going on continuously and imperceptibly with each and every departure from mechanical regularity; and nothing is gained by describing the rhythmical flexibility of good metrical verse as counterpoint.

A large proportion, probably the great majority, of deviations from strict regularity may well have no particular, specifiable emotional effect at all. They still have a function, simple and obvious but highly important: that of preventing tedium, which long continued repetition of the same pattern produces:

> He despises, he shuns me! The thunderbolt falls
> On the rock-seated castle, and crumbles its walls:
> The whirlwind destroys with its furious breath,
> The lightning is charged with its mission of death;
> But the Tempest that scatters my hopes in the air,
> More terrible far, bids me live and despair.
> He despises, he shuns me! There's guilt on my name,
> It drives me to madness; it brands me with shame.
> (*The Letters of Charles Dickens*, ed. House and Storey, vol. I, p. 177)

Even this doggerel (by Dickens at the age of twenty-four), with its intolerably tedious jogtrot, does deviate at a few points from metrical regularity.

It would be wrong to say that in more competent verse we expect the regular repetition of a stress pattern and then get a stimulating surprise; as I have pointed out, we are in fact expecting variety, though without foreseeing its precise form (at least until we have become well acquainted with the poem). This expected but unpredictably executed variation on an emphatically suggested metrical scheme is what Swinburne produced with such staggering facility:

> When the hounds of spring are on winter's traces,
>     The mother of months in meadow or plain
> Fills the shadows and windy places
>     With lisp of leaves and ripple of rain;
> And the brown bright nightingale amorous
>     Is half assuaged for Itylus,
> For the Thracian ships and the foreign faces,
>     The tongueless vigil, and all the pain.

Or take the third line in successive stanzas of 'The Triumph of Time':

> The singing seasons divide and depart...
> Had you eaten and drunken and found it sweet...
> We, drinking love at the furthest springs...
> Grief collapse as a thing disproved...
> Though we seek life through, we shall surely find...
> Rapid and vivid and dumb as a dream...

In terms of conventional scansion the variability is so great that it would be arbitrary to select one or two lines and decide that they alone represent the basic metre from which the others deviate. The exceptions are very much more frequent than the imaginary rule.

To speak of the pleasure given by variation, or the avoidance of the tedium that unchanging repetition of the same rhythmical pattern would produce, is implicitly to take an unfashionable point of view. It implies that the rhythmical pattern itself is providing satisfaction, with rather more satisfaction when variations refresh the metrical set and increase its complexity without obliterating it. It suggests a parallel with the pleasure we can get from a visual pattern, say on a dress fabric or a wall paper, or from a pattern of movement in a dance. And this of course comes perilously close to the conception of metre as a 'superadded attraction' which several generations of critics have anxiously avoided. That they have had good reason to distrust it is evident from some of the early pages of Catherine Ing's book on the Elizabethan lyrics. She notes first that it is 'unlikely that Elizabethan lyrics will give much reward to the seeker after deep and original thought, subtle psychology, strange imagery, or social or philosophical implications in literature... The fact of their existence might be studied as having social or psychological significance, but the poems themselves will usually yield up no such significance.' And then she adds 'This is in itself a major reason for studying them, once their beauty is allowed. They are a supreme test of whether readers appreciate art as art...our enjoyment is dependent on our appreciation of that in the poem which is truly the result of the poet's art' (pp. 21–2).

A more fatally trivializing conception of the poet's art is difficult to imagine. It does less than justice to the emotional quality and sensitiveness to human experience even of some of the lyrics she analyses. And, fortunately, she does by implication free herself from this constricting posture in the greater part of the book. Thus she writes, in objecting to the acrostic poems in Tottel's *Miscellany*, 'If the number of lines in the poem is dictated by a parlour-trick for the sight, and no reason for that number can be grasped without co-operating in the trick, then this part of the metrical construction is not controlled by the rhythmical or emotional intent, and cannot therefore perform metre's function of revealing this intent. It need not be taken seriously.' (p. 88)

None the less the main part of her study treats metrical composition as if it were one of the formal decorative arts; she shows the metrical relation of one part of the poem to other parts, the variations consistent with a maintenance of the broad pattern, and the diversity achieved within unity. The metrical art she describes is, in this aspect, comparable to an appropriate design, painted or incised, on a ceramic bowl or pot. And there need be no objection to this further attraction. If 'superadded attraction' – Wordsworth's term and not used by him derogatively – suggests 'afterthought' it is of course misleading: the form and the decoration of a ceramic may have been conceived as a whole from the beginning, just as the metre and words and feeling of a poem may be. We need not shrink from seeing the metre as an additional attraction, an organizing pattern that offers some satisfaction in itself.

This, however, in relation to the whole range of the poet's art is a small thing, and in some of the finest poetry the formal or decorative value of the metrical scheme is negligible. It is certainly not the kind of satisfaction Shakespeare offers in his later verse. The idea that it ought to be there, that an iambic pentameter must somehow be discovered in each of his lines, led nineteenth and early twentieth century editors and scholars to strange conclusions. In 1902, for example, Van Damm and Stoffel firmly maintained that apart from feminine endings there literally were no syllables beyond the regulation number in any of Shakespeare's lines; the apparent exceptions could all be explained by contractions in pronunciation or – when all else failed – as misprints. The years around the turn of the century seem to have been the heyday for this kind of thing. More seriously misleading, because less bizarre, was the apologetic attitude of editors to irregularities in the verse of the later plays, irregularities that nowadays seem much less troublesome and often of the greatest value.

The unusually long or unusually short line probably gives least difficulty of any when we read or hear Shakespeare. Yet Dover Wilson (1921) assumed that wherever a short line occurred, a broken line as he called it, he had presumptive evidence that a cut had been made during the hasty revision which, according to him, produced the present form of *The Tempest*. Fortunately he was quite inconsistent and accepted some short lines as being what Shakespeare originally meant them to be, for instance when Prospero says

> And deeper than did ever plummet sound
> I'll drown my book

or when he addresses Alonso whose frenzy is checked as he enters the charmed circle:

> A solemn air, and the best comforter
> To an unsettled fancy, cure thy brains,
> Now useless boiled within thy skull: there stand,
> For you are spell-stopped.

Of this last short line he writes 'This broken line is too effective not to be intentional'.

But other short lines he rejected out of hand. When Prospero asks Ariel if he has 'Perform'd to point the tempest that I bade thee?' Dover Wilson takes it that a cut has occurred because Ariel's reply begins with a short line, a short line which in fact serves admirably to introduce the item by item record of the electric storm:

> To every article.
> I boarded the king's ship; now on the beak
> Now in the waist, the deck, in every cabin,

> I flamed amazement. Sometimes ild divide
> And burn in many places; on the topmast...

Another short line, which Dover Wilson says 'points to a glaring "cut"', is specially effective as part of a staccato interchange of annoyance between Prospero and Ariel:

> *Ariel.*                              ...thou didst promise
>    To bate me a full year.
> *Prospero.*                    Dost thou forget
>    From what a torment I did free thee?
> *Ariel.*                    No.
> *Prospero.*   Thou dost: and think'st it much to tread the ooze
>    Of the salt deep;
>    To run upon the sharp wind of the north,
>    To do me business in the veins o' th' earth
>    When it is baked with frost.
> *Ariel.*                    I do not sir.

The fact is that Shakespeare could merely have omitted the short line 'Of the salt deep' if he had wanted regularity; 'to tread the ooze' would have been no more obscure than many passages he left for the commentators. The passage runs quite intelligibly without it, giving a smoother speech with a cumulative and continuous effect but without the hammerblows of annoyance that the half line helps to provide. Whether the short line was in an original version or reached through revision, Shakespeare evidently rated metrical regularity below the effect he gained by his sharper rhythm.

Extra syllables equally disturb Dover Wilson. Prospero is telling Sebastian and Antonio that he knows of their foiled attempt at assassination:

> *Prospero.*   I here could pluck his highness frown upon you
>    And justify you traitors; at this time
>    I will tell no tales.
> *Sebastian.*                    The devil speaks in him.
> *Prospero.*                              No.

Dover Wilson remarks 'The extra-metrical and detached "No" given to Prospero at 1. 130 is curious and can best be explained by a "cut" in the text which deprived us of the rest of the retort.' This comment is especially odd since the line, read with ordinary speech rhythm, has the regulation five beats:

> I will téll   no táles.   The dévil   spéaks in him.   Nó.

It looks as though Dover Wilson was so tied to the metrical foot that he scanned Sebastian's sentence

The dév / il spéaks / in hím

instead of giving it the natural exclamatory rhythm. And when of another passage he remarks 'Correct lining and scansion are impossible' one is reminded of William Thomson's dictum, 'Phrasing is not rhythm, but the two work and vary in harmony with each other; scansion is neither, and it is death to both'.

It is where the simple iambic beat of the verse is disturbed that the earlier editors found most difficulty. For example, K. Deighton in his old Arden edition (1906) of *Troilus and Cressida* was unable to accept one of the lines in Ulysses' speech about the big-brotherly watchfulness of the state:

> The providence that's in a watchful state...
> Keeps pace with thought, and almost, like the gods,
> Does thoughts unveil in their dumb cradles.

Commenting on the last line he writes 'A large variety of conjectures in amendment of this halting line is recorded by the Cambridge Edd. Clarke not only "can see no necessity for change" but "extremely admires the original expression"!' Deighton feels no need to comment on such an egregious opinion as Clarke's beyond putting an exclamation mark after it.

But this 'halting line' is characteristic of many in *Troilus and Cressida* and even more in later plays, including some in which there can be no comforting suspicion of a corrupt text. We have to believe that Shakespeare wanted them, seriously though they disrupt any simple metrical scheme. In fact he has himself stated the view of verse and metre which the later plays exemplify. Just as Hamlet's exhortation to the travelling players is taken to convey Shakespeare's own distaste for acting that plasters on the emotion, so one can see in a passage of *Henry IV Part I* his views on simple metrical writing, with a demonstrated alternative. In the dispute between Glendower and Hotspur, the Welshman uses mechanically correct metre worthy of Tottel's *Miscellany* in preening himself on his command of elegant English, and Hotspur's contemptuous reply is set in vigorous speech rhythms that sharply disrupt the regular iambic pentameter:

> *Glendower.*   I can speak English, lord, as well as you;
>    For I was trained up at the English court;

> Where being but young, I framèd to the harp
> Many an English ditty, lovely well,
> And gave the tongue a helpful ornament, –
> A virtue that was never seen in you.
> *Hotspur.*   Marry, and I'm glad of it with all my heart:     (127)
> I had rather be a kitten, and cry mew,                        (128)
> Than one of these same metre ballad-mongers;
> I had rather hear a brazen canstick turn'd,
> Or a dry wheel grate on the axle-tree;                        (131)
> And that would set my teeth nothing on edge,
> Nothing so much as mincing poetry; –
> 'Tis like the forced gait of a shuffling nag.   (III, i, 121–35)

This is clearly no accidental contrast, between the nearly regular five-beat iambic lines of Glendower (even to 'framèd') and the vigorous speech rhythms of Hotspur, with many stressed syllables coming in immediate succession (line 131) and several lines (e.g. 127, 128) reading most naturally with only four main stresses.

Admittedly Hotspur's speech is in character, but in view of the striking success of the verse it can hardly be taken merely as an expression of his roughness and scorn of urbanity. It exemplifies a form of theatre verse that Shakespeare continued to write and developed much further in the later plays; for instance in *Cymbeline*:

> These three,
> Three thousand confident, in act as many, –
> For three performers are the file when all
> The rest do nothing, – with this word 'stand, stand',
> Accommodated by the place, more charming
> With their own nobleness, which could have turn'd
> A distaff to a lance, gilded pale looks,
> Part shame, part spirit renew'd...          (V, iii, 28–35)

(These three..., aided by the terrain, bewitching others by their own nobleness – which could have turned a distaff into a lance – gilded pale looks, revived both shame and courage.)

It seems questionable whether verse like this passage can usefully be connected with the five-stress iambic line at all. It has departed from it even further than some of the earlier verse, for instance in *Troilus and Cressida* where, as in the following passage, Shakespeare makes considerable excursions away from regular metre but anchors his listeners to metrical lines at either end:

> For time is like a fashionable host,
> That slightly shakes his parting guest by the hand,
> And with his arms outstretch'd, as he would fly,

> Grasps in the comer: welcome ever smiles,
> And farewell goes out sighing.   O! let not virtue seek
> Remuneration for the thing it was;
> For beauty, wit,
> High birth, vigour of bone, desert in service,
> Love, friendship, charity, are subjects all
> To envious and calumniating time.          (III, iii, 165–74)

The later verse is certainly not iambic pentameter. All that can be said is that it avoids any other regular pattern, so that we are clearly reading something different from, say, *Hiawatha*, or *How They Brought the Good News from Ghent to Aix*, or Drayton's *Agincourt*. That much is true, but the fact remains that you get virtually no clue to the nature of the late Shakespearian rhythms by referring them to the iambic five-stress line.

The only guide to reading his lines remains the natural speech rhythms, determined by sense in the main, though sometimes subtly modified by the line ending. To impose simple metrical readings, as editors in the past have done, is often to spoil rhythms of great dramatic effect. In *The Winter's Tale*, when Paulina expresses contrition for upbraiding Leontes, she says

> I'll not remember you of my own Lord
> Who is lost too: take your patience to you...

One of the early editors, Rowe, patched up the metre by reading 'take you your patience to you', but that smooth iambic continuity completely ruins the heavy effect of three stressed monosyllables in succession, with a pause – possibly a sigh – after the second:

> Who is *lost too*: – *take* your patience to you...

A few lines further on, when Leontes has vowed daily mourning at his wife's tomb and says heavily

> Come and lead me
> To these sorrows

another editor, Hanmer, proposed

> Come and lead me
> To these my sorrows.

The original produces an effect of more depressed finality by giving 'sorrows' the only heavy stress in the rhythmical unit, whereas the metrical emendation offers what seems by contrast an almost jaunty alternation of stress.

The idea that a poet must start with a metrical scheme and deviate from it only by 'licence' died hard, for one thing because many poets have actually done that. There are unfinished poems by Shelley with a gap here and there into which a metrically appropriate word would ultimately have been inserted. Richard Aldington once quoted one of them with mocking exaggeration:

> Oh Mary dear that you were here,
> With your – tum-ti-tum – and clear,
> And your – tum-ti-tum-ti – bosom
> Like a – tum-ti – ivy blossom.

Whatever the exaggeration, it still points to a conception of verse writing that many editors and prosodists have tried hard to apply to Shakespeare's later verse.

The verse of the later plays is difficult to label. The ways in which it is free, faithful to the rhythms of spoken English, are fairly clear, but the equally important ways in which it comes under some control other than the grammatical structure of the language are harder to specify. Possibly T. S. Eliot offers help at this point in the account he gives of the verse of his own plays. Of *The Family Reunion* he wrote (*Poetry and Drama*, 1951):

...my first concern was the problem of versification, to find a rhythm close to contemporary speech, in which the stresses could be made to come wherever we should naturally put them, in uttering the particular phrase on the particular occasion. What I worked out is substantially what I have continued to employ: a line of varying length and varying number of syllables, with a caesura and three stresses. The caesura and the stresses may come at different places almost anywhere in the line; the stresses may be close together or well separated by light syllables; the only rule being that there must be one stress on one side of the caesura and two on the other. (p. 27)

The last point is probably unnecessary in the specification, since there could hardly be a caesura preceded only by light syllables; and I think some of his lines have four stresses rather than three (though with varying degrees of stress it must always be uncertain how much stress constitutes a stress). This scarcely matters for the present purpose. What is important is the suggestion of a line of variable length made up of a small number of rhythmical units – units of speech rhythm – each of which has a strong stress and a variable number of lightly stressed syllables, or occasionally one or more heavy stresses only.

The number of main stresses in the line is not at all rigidly controlled. In Ulysses' speech to Achilles, in *Troilus and Cressida*, of which I have already quoted part, the length of line and the number of stresses vary markedly without making the speech in the least unacceptable rhythmically:

> For emulation hath a thousand sons
> That one by one pursue: if you give way,
> Or hedge aside from the direct forthright,
> Like to an enter'd tide they all rush by
> And leave you hindmost;
> Or, like a gallant horse fall'n in first rank,
> Lie there for pavement to the abject rear,
> O'errun and trampled on: then what they do in present,
> Though less than yours in past, must o'ertop yours;
> For time is like a fashionable host...

Clearly the number of stresses in the line can vary within a wide range – probably from two to six – without altering the characteristic movement of the verse. And although in most lines there is one fairly prominent caesura, there can be more than one pause of about equal value, as for instance in the line

> High birth, vigour of bone, desert in service,

where the pauses after 'birth' and 'bone' are both well marked and it is hardly possible to say that one or other is *the* caesura. In other lines the flow from one rhythm unit to the next keeps all pauses minimal:

> That slightly shakes his parting guest by the hand...

where the continuous flow, with a very slight and doubtfully placed caesura, adds to the suggestion of supercilious casualness. Although in most lines there is a pause prominent enough to divide the line into two parts, this caesura is not (as Eliot seems almost to suggest, and as the verse line itself certainly is) superimposed on ordinary language rhythms. It results simply from reading with the natural rhythms of spoken English, and therefore it may sometimes be prominent, sometimes hardly detectable, and sometimes not to be distinguished with any certainty as being more strongly marked than another pause in the same line.

In the same essay in *Poetry and Drama* Eliot suggested that the failure of nineteenth century poets when they wrote drama was 'due largely to their limitation to a strict blank verse which, after extensive use for non-dramatic poetry, had lost the flexibility which blank verse must have if it is to give the effect of conversation' (p. 24). And he thought that in writing modern theatre verse the first thing was to avoid any echo of Shakespeare. But it was a falsely simplified conception of Shakespearian verse that the nineteenth century imitated; and it was Shakespeare himself who showed, in the later plays, how to avoid 'Shakespearian' echoes.

# 5

## Rhythms of irregular verse

Shakespeare's late verse was his furthest departure from those same metre ballad mongers like Glendower, whose ideals had reached decisive fulfilment in Tottel's *Miscellany*. It was, however, nothing like a return to the form of versification against which the Tottel style of smoothness was a reaction. The fifteenth century and early Tudor situation in verse, preceding the Elizabethan establishment of metrical regularity as the norm, was complex, or possibly uncertain and confused. In trying many years ago to understand Wyatt's rhythms I found (Harding, 1946) that orthodox scholarship still accepted the nineteenth century view that his 'roughnesses' were a hangover from the faulty verse of such fifteenth century poets as Hawes and Barclay, which in turn was held to be part of an extraordinary loss of skill that put regular metres beyond the reach of English writers from Chaucer's death until the new wave of regular versification that followed Wyatt and Surrey.

I was able to show without difficulty that some of Wyatt's departures from smooth metre were undeniably intentional, and I suggested that much of his work had its place in the strong English tradition, going back to alliterative verse, of a line that falls into two parts with a pause dividing them. Raymond Southall (1964) in his excellent study of Wyatt confirms that view and develops it in a scholarly and sensitive way; and Ian Robinson (1971) in his stimulating discussion of Middle English verse emphasizes the importance of the half-line as a rhythmical unit. I also suggested that Wyatt came at a turning point when flowing metrical verse was moving towards a supreme place in English poetry but when the other, pausing verse line was still an acceptable alternative as a mode of rhythmical organization. John Thompson (1961) finds earlier examples of a fusing of the two forms of verse line in some of the work in *A Mirror for Magistrates*, for instance *Edward IV* (dated uncertainly as about 1483); it is, he says, in 'a kind of verse that has no name. It has features of two systems of metre, that based on the four-beat line and that based on the line of iambic feet. It belongs to neither; it may be a link between them that shows how and why the old gave way to the new.' (pp. 37–8) He gives as examples of the four stress line from *Edward IV*

> Where was in my life     such an one as I,
> While Lady Fortune     with me had continuance...

commenting that in its pattern of stresses and pause it resembles the Middle English and Old English alliterative line.

Some fusion of two differing modes of verse, or some wavering between them, is certainly more credible than a simple loss of metrical skill in the fifteenth century. Even the earlier scholars had their doubts about the story of a lost skill. Saintsbury (1908, *Cambridge History of English Literature*), who must have done as much as anyone to establish the view of fifteenth century poets as writers of a barbarous pseudo-verse, himself admitted that the supposed facts present a puzzle that has not been entirely explained. After referring to the futility of trying 'to get the verses of Lydgate, Occleve and the rest into any kind of rhythmical system, satisfactory at once to calculation and audition' – unlike the last-ditch prosodists he does at least include 'audition' – he goes on 'And yet we know that almost all these writers had Chaucer constantly before them and regarded him with the highest admiration; and we know further, that his followers in Scotland managed to imitate him with very considerable precision. No real or full explanation of this singular decadence has ever yet been given; probably none is possible'.

He offers two partial explanations. One is the familiar story of the syllabic final '-e' and its obsolescence. The notion is still repeated from one scholar to another that language changes of this kind, as the Romance forms gave way, made the pronunciation of Chaucer a mystery until Victorian scholars rediscovered it. John Thompson (1961), for instance, remarks (pp. 2–3) that Wyatt could not have fully understood Chaucer's iambic pentameter; and he quotes F. N. Robinson, the American editor of Chaucer, 1933; 'It is because this knowledge [of the older pronunciation and grammatical forms] was lost from the fifteenth century down to the middle of the nineteenth that many of Chaucer's most enthusiastic admirers among English poets and critics have regarded his metre as irregular and rough'. It taxes credulity to suppose that at a time when oral communication was so important compared with written, and when carols and nursery rimes kept alive a fairly simple form of metrical language, such a complete lapse in knowledge of the older pronunciation could occur in less than a hundred years. And moreover the Scottish poets of the same period were miraculously spared this linguistic amnesia. Some better story than this is needed.

The second of Saintsbury's partial explanations of the 'singular decadence', a widespread revival at this time of alliterative accentual verse, seems much more to the point, especially if we have in mind John Thompson's suggestion that some of the verse combines features of the flowing iambic line and the four beat pausing line. Where to us the flowing line, with a light caesura, and the pausing line with its point of interruption and pivoting seem quite different modes of rhythmizing they may not have seemed so clearly set apart to fifteenth century writers. And in fact the pausing line and the flowing line could always be juxtaposed, even in alliterative verse such as *Piers Plowman*:

> For hunger hiderward · hasteth him faste,
> He shal awake with water · wastoures to chaste.

In the first line the pause mark only emphasizes what might be the caesura in a flowing line, but in the second it divides rhythmical units that are sharply disjunct. And the couplet that follows this one shows also that the usual four stress line could readily be varied by ordinary speech rhythm to take five stresses:

> Ar fýve yére be fulfílled · suche fámyn shal arýse,
> Thorwgh flódes and thourgh fóule wéderes · frútes shal fáille...
> (Passus VI, 323–6)

(I have accented naturally stressed syllables.)

Against this background it seems a little less puzzling that poets failed to commit themselves to a clearly defined metrical shape for each line. Since in the fifteenth century they were using verse as the vehicle for sermons, political discussions, scientific and medical dissertations, fiction and narrative, it is understandable that they used a form of verse not too decorative for ordinary statement even though capable of being modulated into something more emotive or emphatic. We may find little interest in what they did (perhaps because none of them would have been outstanding in any mode of writing), but their loss of rhythmical quality is not as extreme as one would gather from a nineteenth century critic like Saintsbury. Some examples of what he calls doggerel are far from being as futile, rhythmically, as he finds them, especially when they occur in plays, where the varying movement of speech rhythm has special claims. He quotes an example from the end of the period, in Heywood's *Husband, Wife and Priest*:

> But by my soul    I never go to Sir John
> But I find him    like a holy man,
> For either    he is saying his devotion,
> Or else    he is going in procession...

where the effect is of emphatic repudiation and a hasty mustering of evidence. (I have exaggerated the slight pauses that divide the rhythmical phrasings.) But Saintsbury (1908, *Cambridge History of English Literature*) says the first two lines are pseudo-octosyllabics, and then complains that 'the very next lines slide into pseudo-heroics'. Continuing with this irrelevant labelling he gives from Bale's *Kyng Johan* an example of what he calls pseudo-Alexandrines:

> Monkes, chanons and nones    in divers colours and shape,
> Both whyte, blacke, and pyed,    God send their increase yll happe.

The effectiveness of this vigorous writing depends on our accepting the principle of a pause between rhythmical phrases, even if only the very slight pause needed for us to unify the phrase in our subjective rhythmizing. The pause produces what Saintsbury particularly disliked and called the 'broken-backed line'. He quotes an example from Hawes:

> The mind of men    chaungeth as the mone,

where again only the arbitrary demand for a continuous flow could make the rhythm seem unsatisfactory.

The fact that the men who wrote like this had a great admiration for Chaucer but, unlike their Scottish contemporaries, did not adopt his fairly (but far from completely) smooth verse line seems most naturally to imply that they were essaying something else. John

Speirs (1954), speaking of Scottish Chaucerian poetry of the latter half of the fifteenth century, makes the useful suggestion that 'this kind of poetry may also have been still something of a novelty in the North, something fairly recently transplanted; Chaucer's poems were perhaps being read more freshly by Northerners' (p. 54). This suggests that in England by contrast the Chaucerian verse forms were becoming a little staled by familiarity; and if so, the post-Chaucerians may have been groping for some greater range and freedom in verse. Their reaction was obviously not as vehement as the 'free verse' revolt in the early twentieth century against the Romantic and Tennysonian metres, for it was consistent with an admiration for what Chaucer had done; but the need to do something different may have been felt. The problem remains and must be largely a problem for scholars of the period; but the chances of greater understanding will be improved if the scholarship is pursued within a framework of reasonable psychological and critical assumptions, discarding the idea of a wholesale loss of a metrical skill for a century or more, and relinquishing the critical conviction that a flowing line of verse in a recognized metre is what every poet would write if he could.

It remains true that much of the verse written in the fifteenth and early sixteenth centuries is difficult to rhythmize with any satisfaction. I think that during the transition to the Elizabethan mode of smoothly flowing metre some of the clumsy rhythms may have resulted from a conception that a verse line consisted essentially in a fixed number of syllables, without regard to patterns of differentiated stress. This complicating conception may have been specially influential in translations. Wyatt's sonnets, modelled on Italian poems, have many lines of this kind, with the syllabic count (of ten or twelve) scrupulously observed but the rhythmical patterns apparently given second place, for instance:

> Though I my self be bridilled of my mynde,
> Retorning me backeward by force expresse,
> If thou seke honor to kepe thy promes,
> Who may the hold, my hert, but thou thy self unbynd?
> Sigh then no more, syns no way man may fynde
> Thy vertue to let, though that frowerdnes
> Of ffortune me holdeth; and yet, as I may gesse,
> Though othre be present, thou art not all behinde.

Even very much later, in 1603, Florio's translation of Montaigne suggests the same principle at work when quotations from verse (chiefly Latin) are put into English verse form. Some run smoothly –

> The face with anger swelles, the veines grow blacke with blood,
> The eyes more fiercely shine than Gorgons fierie moode

– where the syllabic count accompanies a simple pattern of alternating stress. But very many cheerfully sacrifice any organization by stress differentiation while scrupulously maintaining the uniform number of syllables (with elision marks if necessary to put things right):

> That you to th'countrie give a man, 'tis acceptable,
> If for the countrie fit you make him, for fields able,
> Of peace and warre for all achievements profitable.
> (both quotations from 'Of Anger and Choler')

Or

> Since that part of my soule riper fate reft me,
> Why stay I heere the other part he left me?
> ('Of Friendship')

Or again,

> The miserable first essayes of youth
> And hard beginnings of warre that ensu'th.
> ('Cowardize the Mother of Cruelty')

Some vestige of this idea that the syllable count makes the metre is implied in the eighteenth and nineteenth century use of the term 'octosyllabics', although of course by this time it was tacitly taken that the eight syllables should be alternately light and heavy in stress.

The notional norm of rhythmical units continuously flowing into one another within a metrical framework was accepted by poets for four hundred years or more, whatever saving irregularities they introduced by 'licence'; and it was against the tenacious conviction that this was the only way to write verse that Gerard Manley Hopkins had to struggle. Understandably, with respected friends writing orthodox verse, he was not content to produce his remarkable rhythms and leave them to speak for themselves; his friends' ears were not attuned to speech of that kind. He therefore worked out in his Preface to the *Poems*, his elaborate prosodic defence of a practice that must in reality have come about spontaneously through his magnificent control of the rhythms of the language. In his account of his versification what I have called the flowing rhythm of regular metre is described as running rhythm, and is said to be 'measured by feet of either two or three syllables and...never more or less' – a position that would be clear and simple if it were not for Hopkins' parenthesis: '(putting aside the imperfect feet at the beginning and end of lines and also some unusual measures, in which feet seem to be paired together and double or composite feet to arise)'. With this parenthesis it becomes evident that his main statement, like most in English prosody, enunciates a fiction rather than a fact of practice. It is first made, and then nullified by reservations and provisos.

Running rhythm, he goes on, would become tame if its regularity were constantly maintained, and reversed feet are therefore often employed, feet in which the stressed and the unstressed syllables change places. This again is familiar prosody. He goes further, however, in saying that if such a reversal is repeated in two feet running (especially if they include the sensitive second foot of the line) a new rhythm is superinduced or mounted upon the old, and since we imagine the old rhythm while hearing the new this device gives something rather like counterpoint in music. Milton, he says, wrote the choruses of *Samson Agonistes* in counterpoint rhythm throughout, 'but with the disadvantage that he does not let the reader clearly know what the ground-rhythm is meant to be, and so they have struck most readers as merely irregular'. However, in his next sentence Hopkins shows that he regards this as no great disadvantage, for he writes, 'And in fact if you counterpoint throughout, since one only of the counter rhythms is actually heard, the other is really destroyed or cannot come to exist, and what is written is one rhythm only and probably Sprung Rhythm...' He thus virtually abandons the idea of counterpoint which, as I have already suggested, is a very improbable explanation of the effect of deviations from regular metre.

'Sprung rhythm' is his term for the rhythm in which he wrote. It is, he says, measured in feet of from one to four syllables, the first syllable being stressed and the others weak; and 'the feet are assumed to be equally long or strong and their seeming inequality is made up by pause or stressing'. But since he adds that one, two or three weak syllables can be added to a foot it becomes clear that his kind of foot is very different from anything the stricter prosodists would recognize. How his nominal prosody helps in the reading of his verse and why his verse should need formal prosodic justification it is not nowadays easy to see. The metrical rationalization shows threadbare when Hopkins goes on, 'Sprung Rhythm is the most natural of things. For (1) it is the rhythm of common speech and of written prose, when rhythm is perceived in them . . .'

This seems to be the basic fact. Instead of the prosodic ingenuities, we can start from the simpler conception of rhythmical units in speech and written prose which sometimes flow into one another in the way I have suggested and sometimes stand relatively isolated and salient on account of speech pauses. The length and structure of these units will vary a great deal. One can if one wishes decide arbitrarily with Hopkins to call the main stress of each unit the first syllable of a foot, but nothing will be gained. Similarly one can if necessary agree with him that every such unit of rhythm consists either in a stressed syllable alone or in a stressed syllable followed by one, two or three relatively weak syllables, to which on occasion may be added one, two or three further weak syllables (his so-called 'outrides'). Nobody could ask for a more flexible prosody. The difficulty is to conceive of any piece of speech or prose that could possibly violate such rules; and consequently it can throw no light on the particular achievement of verse such as Hopkins wrote.

Much of his verse shows his determination to be free from the demand for metrical regularity and flowing rhythm. He drew attention to the fact that *Piers Plowman* is in a different rhythm – what he called sprung and I have called pausing rhythm – and he thought that this kind of rhythm had not been used since the Elizabethan age, 'Greene being the last writer who can be said to have recognised it'. With freedom from the ordinary metrical norms, however, Hopkins still sought very firm constraints through his riming and through his adherence to roughly the same length and rhythmical structure for each line of a poem. He was far from welcoming the extent of freedom that the later free verse writers claimed.

For them, verse consisted essentially in a succession of lines, long or short, each organizing a number of smaller units of speech rhythm (or comprising one unit only), the lines themselves being organized into a larger rhythmical unit consisting of a verse paragraph or a short poem. They believed that this was enough, that natural speech could be shaped into effective verse without metre or rime or standardized shapes for the lines and stanzas. The appeal of free verse as a technique was reinforced by impatience with the distortions of natural speech adopted for the sake of metre – the inversions, the syllabic 'èd' of the past tense, the overuse of auxiliaries, often the archaic ones like 'doth', the distortions of sense and vocabulary in the interest of the metrical scheme. It was, not entirely perhaps but very largely, an accident that free verse as a technique of rhythmical writing was associated in the early years of the century with the doctrines of imagism. And it was unfortunate that the greater part of the free verse produced by the imagist poets was in other respects so anaemic that the effectiveness of its rhythms can hardly be assessed. With its general feebleness in mind one can readily agree with Graham Hough (1960) that 'we nearly always feel in free verse a certain tenuity and slightness of rhythm...' (p. 104), though I reject his view that this results from the absence of any interplay between two rhythms, one provided by 'the syntactic structure' and the other by 'the ideal metrical norm'.

At this point Hough asks the question which is absolutely basic: 'What makes a free verse line a line at all?' To give a satisfactory answer to that question is I believe an essential task for the understanding of rhythm in verse. Hough's answer is that the free verse line 'has no outwardly determined length, as an Alexandrine or an octosyllabic has. It is only a line because it is a rhythmical unit, and it is only a rhythmical unit because it is a unit of sense, a unit of syntax' (p. 103). To my mind this account is mistaken, but its mistakes are of the profitable kind that carry us further into the problem.

In the first place it is not true that the line is a rhythmical unit only because it is a unit of sense and a unit of syntax. Very many free verse lines are certainly not units of syntax, nor of sense unless a single word or any fragment of a possible sentence can be called that. To take examples from two successive pages of H. D.'s *Sea Garden* (1916): 'of the sea'; 'answers'; 'the wind'; 'drench you as they pass'; 'is broken' (pages 40–41). Each of these is a line, but although they are recognizably English and parts of possible sentences they are not in themselves units of sense or syntax.

The free verse line, then, is a unit for some other reason. Hough says that it is a line only because it is a rhythmical unit, but prose (and verse too) has innumerable rhythmical units which are not lines. The converse is nearer the truth, that a phrase or part of a phrase or a succession of phrases is given a special rhythmic unity – or its rhythmic form made salient – by being set apart as a line. The line invites us to find in the succession of words a rhythmical unity beyond what they would have in a passage of prose; or, in a very short line, to experience more saliently the speech rhythm of the word or phrase. At least this is what much free verse evidently intends, as for instance Lawrence's in *Birds, Beast and Flowers* (from which Graham Hough takes 'Snake' for a very sensitive analysis). The shift between short and long lines, and the interruption of a sense clause by a line ending, seem to imply this purpose:

> The involved voluptuousness of the soft-footed cat
> Who is like a fur folding a fur,
> The cat who laps blood, and knows
> The soft welling of blood invincible even beyond bone or metal of bone.

> The soft, the secret, the unfathomable blood
> The cat has lapped
> And known it subtler than frisson-shaken nerves,
> Stronger than multiplicity of bone on bone
> And darker than even the arrows of violentest will
> Can pierce, for that is where will gives out, like a sinking
>
>> stone that can sink no further.
>
>                     ('He-Goat')

The line divisions may not always achieve much, but they very evidently aim at doing something other than merely emphasizing the divisions that sense or sentence structure would impose. Robert Lowell starts a section of a poem with three lines that only bring out more clearly the rhythmical units we should adopt if we read the words as prose:

> I was five and a half.
> My formal pearl gray shorts
> had been worn for three minutes.

But the next sentence, a perfectly straightforward prose statement, has been divided into four and a bit line units not corresponding to sense units:

> My perfection was the Olympian
> poise of my models in the imperishable autumn
> display windows
> of Rogers Peet's boys store below the State House
> in Boston. Distorting drops of water
> pinpricked my face in the basin's mirror.
>
> ('My Last Afternoon with Uncle Devereux Winslow', *Life Studies*)

Here it could certainly be claimed that the line division contributes to the self-mockery. It may be arguable whether it does much, and whether a different lineation might have served equally well, but at least the rhythm given by the lines alters what the syntactic structure would have suggested if the sentence had been printed as prose.

Line endings in one of Charles Brasch's poems mark mainly sense divisions but give at the same time clear directions for pauses, and for continuities, which the same statement in continuous prose might not so evidently demand:

> Tears are our songs today
> Sighing and tears
> The panting of the runner and the sobbing blood
> The heart silence of the homeless,
> Affliction that dare not look round the next bend of time
> Mistrusting even the day to come;
> We who ask the uses of our power
> And whose the kingdom we inherit
> And where the seat of wisdom.
>
> These are the songs of Zion
> Sung in every estranged land.
> ('Bred in the Bone', *Ambulando*)

Something of the same kind may be seen in some of Marianne Moore's free verse poems, where she very deliberately brings out the effectiveness of prose rhythms by giving them line form. So in her account of Eve in Eden she quotes from Richard Baxter, *The Saints' Everlasting Rest*:

> describing it
> as 'that strange paradise
> unlike flesh, stones,
> gold or stately buildings,
> the choicest piece of my life;
> the heart rising
> in its estate of peace
> as a boat rises
> with the rising of the water';
> ('Marriage')

and in 'An Octopus' she tries to bring out the rhythmic value of passages from guide books to the Rockies:

> Is 'tree' the word for these things
> 'flat on the ground like vines'?
> some 'bent in a half circle with branches on one side
> suggesting dust-brushes, not trees;

some finding strength in union, forming little stunted groves,
their flattened mats of branches shrunk in trying to escape'
from the hard mountain 'planed by ice and polished by the wind' –
the white volcano with no weather side;
the lightning flashing at its base,
rain falling in the valleys, and snow falling on the peak –
the glassy octopus symmetrically pointed,
its claw cut by the avalanche
'with a sound like the crack of a rifle,
in a curtain of powdered snow launched like a waterfall'.

Although the line division may interrupt and alter the flow suggested by the sentence structure and the natural runs and pauses of
speech, it justifies itself by producing a rhythm that could be speech
(in some register) and is effective as speech. The wishy-washiness of
much free verse is due not to its freedom but to its lack of compression and its failure to find rhythmically compelling phrases. The
rhythmically compelling phrase is effective in prose or metre or free
verse. When Thersites plans to let Patroclus know that Cressida is
an easy lay he exclaims 'The parrot will not do more for an almond
than he for a commodious drab', and we may for a moment wonder
whether this is prose or two variant lines in Shakespeare's verse. And
it could be free verse. Succinct and forceful as an expression of contempt and distaste, based on a proverbial expression, it has itself the
rhythmical compactness of a proverb.

To speak of free verse is of course a rough and ready way of
pointing towards something which cannot be neatly delimited. No
sharp line will divide all free verse from all verse that could be
claimed as metrical. Graham Hough suggests that 'Prufrock',
'Gerontion', and 'The Waste Land' show simply an extension of the
liberties normal in English verse, and while readily agreeing with
that one can see that when the same process is carried a step or two
further someone will ask at what point an extension of normal
liberties becomes freedom. T. S. Eliot said there was no such thing
as free verse, but since that was in an essay entitled 'Reflections on
Vers Libre' we may guess that he expected people to know more or
less what he was going to write about.

Whatever their limitations, the free verse writers have brought
about a decisive break with the compulsion to justify all verse rhythm
as a variant of metre. In the successful forms of free or less regular
verse the characteristic effects are gained by the controlled interplay

of several modes of unification, several means by which sequences of words can be held together and kept in some degree distinct from other sequences of words, though often flowing easily into them. There are the nuclear rhythmical units, the phrase or sense units, the line units, the syntactical units, and together they contribute to the larger units of paragraph or sub-paragraph. It is the interplay of the line unit with the other modes of unification that distinguishes the organization of free verse from that of prose. This may seem an unforgivable announcement of the obvious, since the lines provide the glaring difference between prose and free verse. But the importance of what is obvious has often been overlooked. To complain that free verse is just prose chopped up into lines ignores the fact that all the prose we ever read is chopped up into lines; we rightly pay no attention to them. But the line of free verse demands attention, not as a typographical whim but as the outline of a rhythmical unit which interacts with other language patterns.

# 6

# Unsatisfactory rhythms

Examining the nature of the verse line is bound to raise a question that lurks behind all the talk of free verse and of speech rhythms in regular verse but is seldom faced, the question whether there is such a thing as a bad rhythm, a rhythmically unacceptable verse line. Every language sequence must have a rhythm of some sort, and the tendency of modern criticism has been to rally staunchly to the defence of rhythms that the older critics condemned as intolerably irregular and faulty. Is there any limit to what we find satisfactory? And if so why? If simple metrical rules are set aside we are left more nakedly confronting the problem of discriminating between acceptable and unacceptable, good and bad, rhythms in verse.

If we believe that rhythms should be expressive of attitudes and emotions we can then reasonably, if subjectively, object to some as inappropriate, or simply as flaccid and dull and unexpressive. But that kind of objection can be brought – often very easily – against the rhythms of metrically regular verse which scan perfectly and are quite unobjectionable as patterns of stressed and less stressed syllables. Although expressiveness is in the end the most important criterion in assessing literary rhythms it gives no help in deciding why, simply as an organized sequence of speech sounds, a line of verse seems wrong.

A simple point of entry to the problem – though potentially a misleading one – is provided by failures to achieve a metrical intention that the form of the verses clearly announces. They do much for McGonagall; they were once familiar (and can still be met with) in the obituary and memorial verse carried by local newspapers. Metrical lapses of this kind are often combined with false rimes:

> All you that stop to read my stone.
> Consider how soon that I was gone.
> Both old and young a warning take.
> And mend your lives before it is too late.
> (In Memory of Samuel Ely who died 17 March 1820,
> Aged 37 years. Tombstone, St Mary Le Tower, Ipswich)

The wish to produce something metrical and rimed, combined with great ineptitude at reconciling English idiom with a metrical scheme (the other end of the spectrum from Swinburne's terrifying gift), has a long ancestry in English. In the Paston letters Elizabeth Brews even fails to recall what was evidently the metrical form of a proverb, although (as so often happens in these fumblings) she retains the rime. She is encouraging John Paston to persist in marriage negotiations for Margery Brews in spite of an initial setback:

> For, cousin, 'it is but a simple oak,
> That's cut down at the first stroke'.
> (8–14 February, 1476–7)

And in the same month Thomas Kela writes to John Paston on similar lines:

> And I heard my lady say,
> That it was a feeble oak,
> That was cut down at the first stroke.

Margery Brews herself attempts more extensive verse in a letter to John:

> And if ye command me to kepe me true wherever I go
> Iwis I will do all my myght you to love and never no mo.
> And if my friends say that I do amiss, they shall not me let for to do,
> Mine heart me bids ever more to love you
> Truly over all earthly thing.
> And if they be never so wrath, I trust it shall be better in time coming.
> (February, 1476–7)

We must allow for the fact that the women who sent these letters were unable to write and had to dictate them, though this Margery could laboriously sign her name and write a word or two of concluding civilities (Davis, 1971, pp. xxxvii–xxxviii). But other verse letters in the Paston collection (e.g. from John Pympe, end of March, or April, 1477) show a similar wish to write metrical verse, with similar stumbling.

These fumblings towards metre by people who lack verbal facility present no critical challenge and have little relevance to the competent poetry of their period; the nineteenth century, with Tennysonian and Swinburnian dexterities as its ideal, seems none the less to have been the heyday of obituary and memorial verse by the partially literate. At other periods, however, the contrast has been less sharp. The Pastons could have found passages in the reputable poets of their day that would not have seemed altogether unlike their own efforts. And in periods like theirs, and ours, when the prevailing modes of accepted poetry allow great metrical freedom, the distinction between competence and blundering, between the successfully irregular and the slovenly or inept, is harder to draw. Laudable efforts to avoid the triteness and obviousness of the more regular metres, even with their 'licences', can slide imperceptibly into flabbiness, insufficiently defined rhythmical units and shapeless lines that have no unity. Where Shakespeare's late verse was rhythmically taut and sharply organized, remote though it was from a metre the prosodists could count on their fingers, the writing of some of the playwrights of the next twenty years or so became rhythmically enfeebled.

Saintsbury (1908, *History of English Prosody*) gives examples, denouncing them with pugnacious rhetoric but never tackling the question of what makes them unacceptable. It is worth while to examine the passage he quotes from Henry Shirley's *The Martyred Soldier* (1638):

> Methought one evening, sitting on a fragrant verge,
> Closely there ran a silver gliding stream:
> I passed the rivulet and came to a garden –
> A paradise, I should say, for less it could not be,
> Such sweetness the world contained not as I saw.

To take for instance the last line but one, it is evident that the awkwardness is not due to its thirteen syllables; knock off three and it becomes even worse –

> A paradise, I should say, for less it...

The trouble can be located in the two light syllables coming together on either side of the caesura, '...shóuld say, for léss...' If the four words made sense by themselves they could readily form a unit of speech rhythm, like 'éightpence, or léss'. But in Shirley's line that pattern is excluded by the strong attachment of 'should' to the preceding pattern: 'A paradise, I should...', with 'say' left dangling. With the next step in the line the light syllable 'for' is firmly attached by sense to 'less', and there is no hope of combining the lightly stressed 'say' with that nucleus, especially with the comma after 'say'.

As prose, the sequence of words would give little difficulty; we should not be implicitly asked to organize them into the rhythmical unity of a 'line'. As it is we are invited by most of the line to attempt a very simple form of rhythmization, mainly with alternate light and heavy stresses:

A páradise I shóuld... (where even the last syllable of 'paradise' has, through its length, enough prominence not to disturb the iambic beat)

and after the caesura

...for léss it cóuld not bé.

Without the effort for variety made by the interjection of 'I should say' it would be a very dull iambic pentameter:

A paradise, for less it could not be.

It is, in fact, this extremely simple metrical regularity of most of the lines that makes the light syllable 'say' seem rhythmically disturbing by being unattached.

The impression that the trouble stems from the simplicity of rhythm in most of the line is confirmed by the contrasting effectiveness of a line from *Cymbeline*, already quoted (in Chapter 4):

For three performers are the file when all
The rest do nothing – with this word 'Stand, stand'...

As far as the sequence of stressed and unstressed syllables is concerned the Shirley line and the second of the Shakespeare lines present the same problem of two light syllables dividing the caesura:

...shóuld say, for léss...
...nóthing – with thís...

But the Shakespeare line neither approaches nor follows this point with a simple alternation of stress, and there is consequently no iambic set which would lead us to attempt a flowing rhythmical continuity across the caesura:

The rést dó nóthing – // with thís wórd / 'Stánd, / stánd,'...

The parts of the line on either side of the main pause are emphatically disjunct, as they often were in the older pausing verse. None the less, although disjunct and non-symmetrical, they remain balanced parts of a unified line. Why there is this balance, how the line comes to possess rhythmical unity, is difficult to say; the conditions making for balance of this kind are no doubt as complex and difficult to specify as those that produce balance in the composition of a painting. But at least we can say that the contrasting line by Shirley fails because it invites simple continuous rhythmizing and then disrupts it; the simple regularity of the adjacent rhythms is what produces the effect of a hiccup in the middle.

It has to be noticed that the sense determines how the words of a line are grouped into rhythmical sub-units. So in the Shirley line the correction of 'garden' to 'paradise' demands 'I shóuld say', though in another context the stress would be different: 'I should sáy, though I'm not sure...' The sequence of strongly and lightly stressed syllables may be the same in two lines and yet the rhythms be totally different because the sense produces different groupings and therefore different points of pause; for instance

> A páradise / I shóuld say, // for léss it cóuld not bé.
> A céntipede! // I swállowed and chóked, / and drópped the cúp.

The rhythms are so sharply different that it takes a moment to see that the sequential pattern of stressed and unstressed syllables is identical in the two lines. The form of rhythmical organization in a line depends on the relations among its sub-units of speech rhythm.

The challenge to explain an unsatisfactory rhythm is sharpest in free verse, where there can be no temptation to think in terms of permissible and impermissible deviations from a metre. As an example for examination we can look at a passage from a translated poem, reading it first in a prose version:

...about me now O Lord be cool, and when *my* hour has come to pass, and make me pure that from my heart no thought or strident call of words or anything imperfect, ever again in the still glass of my devout contemplation may fall.

As prose it may seem rather clumsy, but it is not as frustrating rhythmically as some parts become in verse:

> ...about me now
> O Lord be cool, and when *my* hour has come to pass,
> and make me pure that from my heart no thought or strident call

of words or anything imperfect, ever again in the still glass
of my devout contemplation may fall.
(C. J. D. Harvey's translation of
The Hound of God by N. P. Van Wyck Louw, from Afrikaans Poems
with English Translations, ed. A. P. Grove and C. J. D. Harvey,
London, 1962)

It is in particular the last line that moves unsatisfactorily. The
word 'contemplation' is difficult to unite rhythmically with either 'of
my devout' or 'may fall'. We could easily make a simple if undistinguished rhythmical line by altering 'contemplation' to some such
word as 'integrity' and preserving the mainly iambic beat of the
earlier lines. But the influence of the previous lines is not really
necessary to make the last unsatisfactory. In prose it would not be too
objectionable: we could say 'the high pitch of my devout contemplation may fall'. Yet once it becomes a verse line it splits inexorably into
three rather jerky units:

ŏf mý dĕvóut   cŏntĕmplátiŏn   mǎy fáll.

Once again, the difficulty cannot be described in terms of the un-
acceptability of the sequence of stressed and unstressed syllables, for
we can use just the same sequence in a different speech rhythm and
make what is at least a united line:

whĕn sóftlý, sílĕnt, thĕ fóliăge stírs.

It is not the sequential pattern of stress but the succession of rhythmical units that matters. A prosodist like Saintsbury would have
named and listed the 'feet' involved and taken it as self-evident or a
matter of immutable doctrine that certain combinations of feet are
metrically disastrous. The question is whether anything more nearly
approaching an explanation is possible.

As in the Henry Shirley line, a crucial part is played by the simple
pattern of alternating stress at the beginning and end of the line, the
iambic

Of mý devóut. . .may fáll.

That creates a strong set, a preparedness to rhythmize in the pattern
dedá, dedá; but this preparedness is frustrated by the rival pattern
dededá, dededá of

. . .contemplátion may fáll.

In the line constructed to use the same sequence of stressed and unstressed syllables, in a different rhythmical grouping, the sense
imposes pauses that break up the pattern dedá, dedá and prevent that
set from forming:

> when sóftly, sílent, the fóliage stírs.

In other words, marked differences of stress pattern in the rhythmical
sub-units within a line are not fatal to the rhythmical unity of the line
so long as uniform rhythmization of the sub-units is not suggested by
the major part of the line and then at some point frustrated. Just what
patterning is invited depends on speech rhythm, with pauses dictated
partly by the auditory and articulatory shape of words and phrases –
the basic usages of English – and partly by the sense. It is these factors
that establish the syllabic groupings that we rhythmize as we read;
and quite diverse rhythmical shapes can be combined in a unified
line if the sense pauses prevent any attempt to find a simple repeating
pattern.

The principle can be illustrated in the rhythmical weakness of
some lines by T. S. Eliot in a poem he contributed to the wartime
propaganda publication, *London Calling* (ed. Storm Jameson, 1942).
In prose layout the passage would run

The enduring is no substitute for the transient, neither one for the other. But the
abstract conception of private experience at its greatest intensity becoming
universal, which we call 'poetry', may be affirmed in verse.

The sense is perhaps a little uncertain but the rhythm is unobjectionable. In its verse form, however, something goes wrong:

> The enduring is no substitute for the transient
> Neither one for the other. But the abstract conception
> Of private experience at its greatest intensity
> Becoming universal, which we call 'poetry',
> May be affirmed in verse.

The trouble lies in the last three lines, especially the fourth.

Here again it is not diversity in the pattern of the component
rhythmical units that causes difficulty but an uneasy compromise or
hesitation between sameness and diversity. The sameness comes
from having three successive lines each with two stresses on either
side of the caesura, with consequently six very similar blocks of
language:

> Neither óne for the óther.
> But the ábstract concéption
> Of prívate expérience
> at its gréatest inténsity
> Becóming univérsal,
> which wé call póetry, . . .

Very likely the intended rhythm for the last phrase was 'whĭch wĕ căll póetry', but by then we have been drilled into iambs and anapaests and find it hard to drop them. And the necessity for dropping them created by the three successive light syllables of 'Becóming ŭnĭvérsal' remains so much an isolated disturbance of the set that we should almost prefer 'Become universal', though the rhythmical repetitiveness would then be more obtrusively dull and mechanical.

This was the period when Eliot in *Four Quartets* offered similar discursive passages of abstract statement, but much more rhythmically diversified, deliberately extending in this direction the range of his effective poetry. With more serious intent than a patriotic exercise could generate he produced rhythms that were as varied and flexible as prose but still so organized that each line is rhythmically a unit, with the transition from line to line providing continuity or rhythmical compatibility, as in the passage quoted earlier:

> . . . This is the use of memory:
> For liberation – not less of love but expanding
> Of love beyond desire, and so liberation
> From the future as well as the past. Thus, love of a country
> Begins as attachment to our own field of action
> And comes to find that action of little importance
> Though never indifferent.

The rhythmical weakness of the passage from 'A Note on Poetry in Wartime' points up by contrast the delicate achievement of these other passages of abstract statement in which patterns of speech are organized into lines which themselves possess rhythmical unity.

The subtlety of the differences in speech movement that can make one rhythm satisfactory and another not may be illustrated from two lines of Shakespeare that would be scanned in the same way but produce very different effects. One occurs in a passage from *Timon of Athens*, the verse of which some scholars (for instance Una Ellis-Fermor, followed by H. J. Oliver in the New Arden edition) have supposed to be at some points only first jottings, a draft that would have been worked up into blank verse later. Certainly some of the verse is weak. Towards the end of Alcibiades' speech to the senate we have the lines

> To kill, I grant, is sin's extremest gust:
> But in defence, by mercy, 'tis most just.
> To be in anger is impiety;
> But who is man that is not angry?
> Weigh but the crime with this.           (III, v, 54–8)

The line 'But who is man that is not angry?' seems to tail off. Obviously it lacks the fifth stress of the preceding lines. But this seems not to be the whole answer, for the similar short line already quoted from *Troilus and Cressida* is altogether more effective:

> [The providence that's in a watchful state]
> Does thoughts unveil in their dumb cradles.

The fact is that although this line would no doubt be conventionally scanned as if it were iambic – 'in théir dumb crádles' – the natural speech rhythm demands three slow and stressed syllables in succession – 'in théir dúmb crádles'. This heavier, more deliberate movement gives the line a roundedness and completeness lacking from the thin, quick movement of 'is not angry'. If this is the crucial difference we ought to be able to make the Alcibiades line more rhythmically complete by altering the syllabic weight:

> But who is man that shuns all anger?

My impression is that this does make the line less trailing and unfinished, even though it still lacks, in conventional scansion, the fifth foot of the pentameter. If so, it further supports the view that the duration of a syllable cannot be excluded from the factors creating the differences of salience that shape the unit of speech rhythm.

Rhythmical completeness in a line is perfectly compatible with its being run on in sense to the next line, so long as timing and intonation preserve the effect of the line ending as a form of punctuation. Natural speech rhythm and sense may suggest a pause that corresponds with the end of the line; or, for special effects, the line ending may modify the usual timing and intonation of a unit of speech and sense. To gain a derisory anti-climax Eliot even uses a run-on stanza:

> Princess Volupine extends
> A meagre, blue-nailed, phthisic hand

> To climb the waterstair. Lights, lights,
> She entertains Sir Ferdinand
>
> Klein...

But it can happen that run-on lines break a speech rhythm in a way that distorts it pointlessly, and it is then necessary either to accept a distortion of the language or to lose the rhythmical wholeness of the line.

Saintsbury (1908, *History of English Prosody*) found this fault extremely disagreeable in the weaker verse of the Jacobean and Caroline playwrights. He quotes (vol. II, pp. 307–8), for instance, from James Shirley, *The Brothers*:

> I know thy poverty, and came not to
> Bribe it against thy chastity; if thou
> Vouchsafe thy fair and honest love, it shall
> Adorn my fortunes which shall stoop to serve it
> In spite of friends or destiny.

He takes the line breaks at 'to', 'thou', and 'shall' to be 'extremely ugly blemishes'. From the same play he quotes

> He had better cool his hot blood in the frozen
> Sea, and rise hence a rock of adamant
> To draw more wonder to the north, than but
> Attempt to wrong her chastity...

and comments 'Here a fight might be made for "but" if it stood by itself; but the neighbourhood of "frozen" with its totally unjustifiable divorce from "sea" is not likely to dispose anyone with an ear to mercy'. A less rigid taste than Saintsbury's would certainly not need to make a fight for the pause at 'but', with the effective emphasis it throws on 'Attempt', but the other breaks he condemns do illustrate the possibility of conflict between language usages and the rhythmical unity of the line.

In more recent poetry the conflict is obvious in the weak lines from Isaac Rosenberg's *Moses*:

> The old clay is broken
> For a power to soak in and knit
> It all into tougher tissues
> To hold life...

where so closely coherent a speech unit as 'knit it all' could not have been successfully broken except for some very special effect; in fact the line break here is a rhythmical nuisance and a prose version would have been more effective: '. . . for a power to soak in and knit it all into tougher tissues to hold life'. For contrast one can take a phrase just as strongly welded together in ordinary speech as 'reach into', but divided by the line ending with complete success in 'Burnt Norton':

> . . . Words, after speech, reach
> Into the silence . . .

where the suggestion of probing deep or extending indefinitely is secured by the prolongation of 'reach' (compared with 'speech') and the reinforcing emphasis on 'Into'.

What I have offered is likely to be far from a full account of the nature of unsatisfactory rhythms. One difficulty in discussing the problem is the inescapably subjective judgement implied in saying that a rhythm is weak or clumsy; but the subjectivity offers no excuse for evading the problem: you may not agree when I say that this or that particular rhythm is weak, but there must be other rhythms that you do regard as weak and you still face the problem of saying why; or, if you should be tempted to say that all rhythms are good and none better than others you are maintaining in effect that rhythm is of no significance. The problem does exist and a full understanding of rhythmical organization in language would include a solution.

It seems clear at least that the verse line as a rhythmical whole is crucial. Great diversity of pattern among the sub-units of rhythm can occur in what is still experienced as a rhythmically coherent line, especially when speech pauses ensure that sub-units are kept disjunct at points where an attempt at continuous flow would disturb the pattern of preceding or succeeding sub-units. What disturbs the rhythmical unity of a line is the creation of a set towards a particular pattern of rhythmizing into which some other part of the line will not fit. It is the speech rhythms suggested by the sense, and by the English accentuation of words and phrases, that shape the rhythmical patterns making up the line; the speech rhythms determine which syllables have to be combined into rhythmical units.

How firmly established a set has to be, how much emphasized by exactness and frequency of repetition before it imposes itself on the whole line, no doubt needs further investigation, and it may well be at this point that individual differences between readers, as well as their familiarity with various types of rhythm, count for most. The mechanisms by which the set is created need to be examined more closely. The descriptive side of this task has to a great extent been done by conventional prosody in specifying 'licences', permissible deviations from the metrical set; observing for instance in which feet of an iambic pentameter an inversion of stress is acceptable and in which it is not. But much more would have to be done before a full and intelligible account could be given of relations among sub-units of speech that go to make up a rhythmizable line. And further questions concern the maximum length of line that can be experienced as a rhythmical unit. Whitman, for example, clearly extended his lines to the limit, or beyond the limit, of what most readers can unify rhythmically; but various devices, especially (as in the Psalms) the repetition of syntactic patterns, contribute to the impression of unified segments of language, though they may not always be rhythmical wholes.

If we believe that some verse rhythms are weak we have to ask how poets come to write them. Naturally, any writer, however good, may have lapses, as in the examples I have quoted from Eliot and Rosenberg. More interesting problems are posed by the periods when feeble and slovenly rhythms have been widely tolerated among accepted writers. Discussing his Jacobean and Caroline examples, Saintsbury (1908, *History of English Prosody*) suggests that the playwrights concerned imitated in a blundering way the irregularities of the more complex blank verse; 'the most perfect blank verse', he says, 'is (from certain points of view) a tissue of exceptions and irregularities'. And he adds, rather vaguely, that in the post-Elizabethan period 'there *was* a spirit of such blundering abroad' (vol. II, pp. 314–15). This is as near as he comes to an explanation. If a spirit of blundering was abroad it was oddly selective, since the period included poets as metrically skilful as Herrick, George Herbert, Suckling, Milton. Saintsbury must have been thinking only of theatre verse. It may well be that then, as in much of the twentieth century, directors had little grasp of the possibilities of rhythmical speaking and allowed their players to ignore the unity of the line. It has been common enough this century to hear players completely dissociating the beginning from the end of a Shakespearian line. There must always be a danger that in a verse play the performers'

techniques of loudness, emphasis, pauses, pitch modulations, gestures, posture and facial expression will swamp the inherent language
qualities of sense, emotional shading through the associations of
words and phrases, and rhythm. The threat to the rhythm is all the
greater when, as in the later Shakespeare plays, the verse deliberately
avoids metrical obviousness; the complex rhythms, perhaps poorly
understood from the first, offered an excuse to later writers for
metrical slovenliness without rhythmical subtlety, an excuse they
took the more readily for knowing how the players would mangle
their lines in any case.

# 7

# Expressive effects of rhythm in verse

From time to time already I have silently assumed that rhythms can have expressive effects – conveying emotion, of course, but other states of mind too, for instance indecision, hesitancy, impetuosity. They may also seem to suggest qualities of the relation between one person and another, the abject, the imperious, the wheedling, and so on. The term 'expressive effects' will serve to cover all such possibilities. Literary critics have regularly assumed that rhythm and metre do have these effects. Yet it is not at all easy to demonstrate that they do, still less how they do it.

The most improbable view has been that metre in general has some specifiable effect on the reader's or hearer's state of emotion. The suggestion is still occasionally to be heard that regular metres have a mildly hypnotic effect, with a consequent heightening of the reader's susceptibility to the emotional suggestions of the words. I have never seen any evidence for this view. It is not enough to argue that because an extreme form of regularly repeated stimulation may induce, or help to induce, the hypnotic trance a very weak and only approximately regular stimulation will have milder effects of the same kind. This would be like arguing that because long sustained noise of high intensity damages our hearing we must be doing it some harm whenever we listen to anything. And it must also be remembered that in the ordinary way the induction of even a mildly hypnoidal state requires concentration on a very simple and monotonously repeated stimulus, in the absence of distracting interests, and that many people, however willing, are very difficult or impossible to hypnotize. Even what we think of as regular metrical verse is far from being quite simply repetitive, it has to be read among all the distractions of a normal environment, and the subject matter of the poem offers further distraction from the repetitive stimulus of the mere sound or imagined speech stresses. It is in the highest degree unlikely that any hypnoidal effect can be an element in the claim that a poem has on the attention of most readers.

If by any chance it were we should face another difficulty. The hypnoidal state involves increased suggestibility, less critical alertness, and a restricted range of awareness. We should face the problem of reconciling this with our ideal of the alert, discriminating reader who relates each part of a poem to the total context and brings to bear the whole range of his values to which the poem may be relevant.

But although the hypnoidal theory is completely improbable it may point to a different truth. The more regular and emphatic metres, from nursery rimes to Swinburne, are at their best satisfying as cunningly constructed patterns of language; and our pleasure as they unfold, with some regularity and some variety, may well make us more easily satisfied with the words that embody them and less inclined to look closely at the aptness of the imagery and metaphor, or critically at the sense, or questioningly at the validity of the suggested emotion. The prose cadences of liturgies probably have the same slightly lulling effect, greatly increased by the factors of habit and customary context, and they are likely to slide soothingly through the mind of the worshipper without always demanding close attention to their meaning. Nothing like hypnosis need be involved. It is rather that we are so well satisfied with one aspect of the phrase or the poem, as we might be with the decorative façade of a building, that we are not so alertly attentive to the rest. In this sense, it is true, we may be lulled by some forms of rhythm and metre – with, very often, consequent problems for discriminating enjoyment.

In practice, however, most critical discussion has rightly assumed that the importance of rhythm lies not in any such generalized effect but is bound up with the highly individual achievement of the poem in which it is embodied. It is not 'rhythm' or 'metre' that matters, but the unique rhythm of the unique poem.

The most challenging view of the expressive importance of particular rhythms arises from the suggestion by poets here and there that a rhythmical pattern of some kind may appear at a very early stage of the creative process, even before the theme of the poem has begun to define itself. 'I know' wrote T. S. Eliot that a poem, or a passage of a poem, may tend to realize itself first as a particular rhythm before it reaches expression in words, and that this rhythm may bring to birth the idea and the image; and I do not believe that this is an experience peculiar to myself. (*The Music of Poetry*)

## A. R. Chisholm (1963) speaks of Valéry's similar report:

In his Oxford lecture, *Poésie et pensée abstraite*, delivered in 1939, Valéry has told us of the relationship that he once noticed between the rhythm of his walking and the rhythm of an as yet unshaped poem. He thus seems to imply (1) that there is an almost physiological element in the making of poetry, and (2) that rhythm precedes words in the genesis of a poem.

In rather more emotive language Virginia Woolf records what seems to have been the same sort of experience:

Now this is very profound, what rhythm is, and goes far deeper than words. A sight, an emotion, creates this wave in the mind, long before it makes words to fit it; and in writing...one has to recapture this, and set this working (which has nothing apparently to do with words) and then, as it breaks and tumbles in the mind, it makes words to fit it.

(L. C. Knights, to whom I am grateful for helpful discussions about rhythm, gave me the references to Valéry and Virginia Woolf. I have not been able to trace the source of the latter quotation.)

Valéry, Eliot and Viginia Woolf were subtle writers giving a retrospective account of extremely complex creative experiences, and we might wonder if they were deceiving themselves. But curious support for this kind of testimony comes from the altogether simpler creative effort of Cole Porter, the popular song writer of the 1920s and 1930s. His biographer George Eells (1967) reports an account of his methods from Abe Burrows, a librettist with whom Cole Porter worked on a musical show. They would agree on the basis of a song that would fit the plot, and later on Porter would telephone Burrows and ask him to listen to the beat he had worked out. 'I understand' says Burrows

from people who saw him when he called – I couldn't, I was on the other end of the phone – that he'd put down the phone and beat it out. Pah-pah-pa-pa-pah – and I'd begin to hum. 'Don't hum, don't hum!' he'd say. What he did was he got himself set with the beat – I never knew any other composer who does this – and that's how he got that unity. He'd do the beat, then match the lyrics to the beat, then write the tune to the lyrics. (pp. 275–6)

No author is likely to recall accurately the precise sequence of events when the nebulous background of the creative act is forming, but although the evidence is meagre and much of it contaminated by being retrospective and produced for an appreciative audience, still it deserves to be kept in mind for the general direction in which it points – the very early stage at which a rhythmical pattern may show itself and begin to have an influence on the emergence of words.

Prompt and unthinking rhythmization of course gives no guarantee of the merit of the writing. Painfully bad poems have been poured out or jerked out under the influence of strong and sincere emotion. Moreover the finality and completeness of a spontaneously emerging rhythmical form must not be exaggerated. A poet may from the start be groping towards a particular rhythm for a passage of verse, but yet not be able to reach it without false moves and revisions; it is more like an elusive word on the tip of our tongue, sufficiently activated to make us reject false approximations but not itself immediately accessible. Thus, although Eliot said that the final part of *The Waste Land* was the sort of writing which, after making no progress for months or years 'may suddenly take shape and word' and in which 'long passages may be produced which require little or no retouch', the facsimile of the early drafts shows that several revisions were sometimes needed before he reached the final rhythm. This is notable in the very fine section beginning 'A woman drew her long black hair out tight' – a magnificent example of the verse paragraph – of which the confidently unfolding rhythmical pattern is, in the final version, an essential feature. The very broad rhythmical movement was there from the start, but it was given infinitely greater assurance, complexity and uninterrupted development through revision. The first version we have runs

> A woman drew her long black hair out tight
> And fiddled whisper-music on those strings
> The Shrill bats quivered through the violet air
> Whining and beating wings.
> A man, distorted/contorted by some mental blight
> Yet of abnormal powers
> Such a one crept/I saw him creep head downward down a wall
> And upside down in air were towers
> Tolling reminiscent bells –
> And [there were] chanting voices out of cisterns and of wells.

The next version is not very different from the final form, but Eliot was still having trouble with the man who was creeping down a wall:

> And bats with baby faces, in the violet light
> Whistled, and beat their wings
> A[man] form crawled downward down a blackened wall...

This not only gave him more of the rounded vowels but cut out the description of the man, which had slowed up the movement of the line. And yet there was still a slight pause at the word 'wings', beyond that required for the line ending, because a new sentence began with the new subject 'A man'. The pause checked the rapid continuity of the lines. The final solution came when Eliot realized that he could cut out not only the description of the man but the man himself and leave the bats to do the crawling:

> And bats with baby faces, in the violet light
> Whistled, and beat their wings
> And crawled head downward down a blackened wall...

This finally achieved the magnificent continuity and cumulative effect of the passage, coming to a climax in the 'reminiscent bells, that kept the hours' and followed by the long decelerating last line,

> And voices singing out of empty cisterns and exhausted wells.

A crucial advantage was gained by avoiding a fresh grammatical beginning with 'A form crawled downward...' The grammatical break had altered the movement of the passage, giving 'wings' a drop in pitch instead of the higher, sustaining pitch which means that the sentence is going on. It is this interaction of sense, grammar, line ending and stress pattern that determines the total movement of a passage.

Complex and delicate in interaction, several different features of language produce effects that may mistakenly be attributed to rhythm. Of these the simplest to identify is the intonation of the words, their melody or pattern of pitch. It responds accurately to the sense in which the words are taken. Consider, for example, Macbeth's lines

> This supernatural soliciting
> Cannot be ill; cannot be good: –

L. C. Knights (1946), endorsed by Muir in his Arden edition, has said of this passage that 'its sickening see-saw rhythm completes the impression of "a phantasm, or a hideous dream"'. The fluctuations of a divided mind are certainly there. Yet, surprisingly, it turns out

not to be the rhythm that produces the sickening see-saw, but intonation, intonation reflecting the sense. Suppose the speaker had been
Banquo, expressing a different view, more likely to have come from
him:

> This supernatural soliciting
> Cannot be good; cannot be good: –

The rhythm is the same, with the same grouping of syllables and the
same distribution of stress within the groups. Yet the effect is totally
altered because the change of sense brings a different intonation for
'cannot' and 'good'; the line now conveys perhaps musing, perhaps
conviction or an effort towards conviction.

The intonation or pitch pattern of a phrase is delicately responsive
to the sense of the words and to the attitude of the speaker to his
hearer; the rhythm, on the other hand, is determined, with much less
variability, by the established pronunciation of the language. A child,
or a foreigner with only a little knowledge of English, could offer the
right patterns of stress and timing for

> Cannot be ill; cannot be good: –

while still not having understood the sense (in context) well enough
to get the appropriate pattern of pitch. (The limitation can be heard
on radio when poorly educated people read from a script.)

Other, and still subtler, features of the spoken language affect the
expressive quality of sentences and phrases. It seems surprising, for
instance, that exactly the same short phrase occurring with the same
rhythm in two blank verse lines should have a different emotional
effect. Yet the phrase 'Give me your hand' has a very different effect
in two Shakespearian contexts. In the quarrel scene in *Julius Caesar*
Brutus admits that he too was ill-tempered and Cassius exclaims

> Do you confess so much? Give me your hand. (IV, iii, 119)

But the emotional effect is entirely different in *The Merchant of
Venice* when Antonio resigns himself to death:

> Give me your hand, Bassanio, fare you well! (IV, i, 264)

Obviously the reader, or the actor, speaks the phrase differently in
the two contexts: the intonation will be slightly different, the stress
on the initial word, 'Give', will be sharper in Cassius's exclamation,
his tempo may be faster, his speaking of the phrase will show a

greater contrast between strong and light stresses than Antonio's, and his utterance of 'hand' will probably be crisper, more staccato, than Antonio's more sustained sound on the same word. Yet all these variations, with their contrasting total effect, are consistent with the same pattern of rhythm. It is just the same in everyday speech; 'Open the door' can vary from an imperious command to an abject plea.

With these complicating subtleties at work it can be no surprise that there are uncertainties in what a critic can convincingly attribute to rhythm. Thus D. G. Gillham (1966), in his extremely sensitive and illuminating study of Blake's *Songs*, gives contrasting descriptions of the rhythms of two poems, 'Spring' and 'The Fly'. Recall the last few lines of each: the ending of 'Spring' runs

> Little lamb,
> Here I am;
> Come and lick
> My white neck;
> Let me pull
> Your soft wool;
> Let me kiss
> Your soft face;
> Merrily, merrily we welcome in the year.

The last two stanzas of 'The Fly' run

> If thought is life
> And strength and breath,
> And the want
> Of thought is death;
>
> Then am I
> A happy fly,
> If I live.
> Or if I die.

'It has a jerky, frivolous rhythm' writes Gillham. But could we be sure of which poem? His response to the rhythm is bound up with, and may have been influenced by, his broad conception of the two poems. He writes 'The description of thought as reflex and self-contained given in "The Fly" is well exemplified by the movement of the poem itself. It has a jerky, frivolous rhythm...' (p. 219) But of 'Spring' he says 'The poem refers to the sporadic activities of different creatures, but the rhythmic pattern reminds us simultaneously of the underlying harmony of their mood and their movement as part of the Season' (p. 205).

In the context of the broad description the difference ascribed to the rhythms seems plausible; and yet, resorting to desecration in the interest of inquiry, we can mingle couplets from the two poems without creating any striking rhythmical anomalies:

> Birds delight
> Day and night
> Then am I
> A happy fly,
> Lark in sky
> Merrily,
> If I live.
> Or if I die.

It would not be worth while considering an example like this if it were not that Gillham is an exceedingly acute and perceptive critic. We may well accept his discrimination between the total effect of the two poems but still doubt whether their rhythms can be so confidently distinguished. After all, 'the sporadic activities of different creatures' in the spring (especially lambs) might quite well strike us, without any implied condemnation, as jerky and frivolous. The probability is that as far as a rhythm has in itself a psychological effect it may be expressive of, or appropriate to, a fairly wide range of states of mind; and conversely several broadly similar rhythms may be appropriate to one and the same state of mind.

The difficulty of deciding how far the expressive quality of a sequence of sounds is due to its rhythm and how far to other properties can certainly be formidable. No doubt a great deal of future work, perhaps experimental, will be needed before we can hope to identify the range and kinds of expressive value that speech rhythm in itself may possess. But some clearing of the ground can be attempted.

The best starting point is the recognition that language rhythm in the sense of patterns of stress and pause is a matter of movement, not simply sound.

Differences of stress are evident even in a whispered sentence lacking any variations of loudness or pitch. As R. H. Stetson (1951) puts it, '...stress is not a matter of the properties of sounds, it is a matter of the coordination and culmination of a movement' (p. 95).

David Abercrombie (1965) in the paper already quoted (in Chapter 1) develops the implications of the physical facts. Having noted that the chest pulses, each making a syllable, are every now and then reinforced to give the stronger stress pulse, he goes on, 'The rhythm of speech is a rhythm of these two systems of pulses... the rhythm is already *in* the air stream, in fact, before the actual vowels and consonants which make up words are superimposed on it' (p. 17). He adds that our perception of speech largely depends on our grasping what the speaker is *doing*: 'As we listen to the sounds of speech, we perceive them not simply as sounds, but as clues to movements'. It is, moreover, because speech rhythm is primarily muscular rhythm that 'verse can be immediately recognized and felt as verse in *silent* reading, which otherwise would not be easy to explain'.

The expressive value of speech rhythm depends on this fact that it is a movement system. It can in the first place, of course, suggest other forms of movement, movements of people and animals most frequently, but also inanimate movement – of trees or water for example – and the time quality of any event, its suddenness, gradualness, acceleration and so on. But a subtler and even more important range of effects arises from the fact that rhythm in speech forms part of the extensive and intimate patterns of bodily movement, including incipient movement and posture, in which the speaker's emotional attitudes express themselves (in which, at least to a great extent, they actually consist).

The simplest possibility is to be seen in verse that aims at suggesting some external pattern of movement, as with Alfred Noyes –

> And the highwayman came riding –
> Riding – riding –

We might do the same sort of thing by jogging a child on our knee. More significant imitative rhythms occur in Rosenberg's poem 'Marching (as seen from the left file)':

> My eyes catch ruddy necks
> Sturdily pressed back –
> All a red brick moving glint.
> Like flaming pendulums, hands
> Swing across the khaki –
> Mustard-coloured khaki –
> To the automatic feet.

Although superficially a simple imitation of movement, in the same category as the highwayman's riding, the rhythm of the last three lines goes a little further, since Rosenberg is concerned in that poem with the mechanized forms of destruction that will obliterate fine human bodies, themselves keyed up by training into automata, and the verse movement reinforces what 'automatic' in the last line conveys.

But more complex possibilities develop when the rhythms suggesting external movement convey at the same time qualities of the speaker's mood and attitude. A fairly obvious example, again from Rosenberg, is the opening of 'Spring 1916' where the rhythm not only accords with the posture and quality of movement he sees in the coming of a wartime spring but at the same time suggests more directly the poet's own sombre attitude and inhibited flow of feeling:

> Slow, rigid, is this masquerade
> That passes as through granite air;
> Heavily – heavily passes.

In such passages as this all that should be claimed is that the rhythm reinforces – or, very often, slightly qualifies – the sense of the words. Independently of the sense it would have a very limited and uncertain significance. We have to avoid any suggestion, on the one hand, that the rhythm makes any part of the sense redundant; on the other, that the emotional stance could have been evoked by words offering the same sense in a different rhythmical form.

A remarkable and sustained use of rhythm to suggest qualities of external movement, fused with the concerns and attitudes expressed by the sense of the words, was achieved by Eliot in a passage of 'The Dry Salvages'. Anne Ridler (1947) writes:

...the subtleties of poetic rhythm are produced by the variations of accent and speed in ordinary speech, and it is the poet's business to use these, not to violate them; or if the rhythm of his line goes against them, to contrive it so rarely and consciously as to produce a double possibility, that marvellous ambiguity which is one of the most complex joys of poetry. (An example of this particular effect is in the movement beginning 'Lady, whose shrine stands on the promontory', in *The Dry Salvages*.)

As a literal statement this is not altogether satisfactory, but it points towards a truth, and she rightly chooses a passage which illustrates it admirably. Essential to its rhythmical effect is the fact that in verse the unity of the line – and with it the line ending – is superimposed on the rhythms of speech. In this passage, 'Lady, whose shrine...', the line endings interrupt the ordinary flow of speech in a way that helps to suggest the uneasy, broken swinging of waves out at sea and ground swell:

> Pray for all those who are in ships, those
> Whose business has to do with fish, and
> Those concerned with every lawful traffic...

where the first two lines have a fairly smooth continuity until the last word in each with its unexpected upswing and poising. (The repeated strokes on 'those' also mark the bell-buoy's clang at irregular intervals in the wave movement.) Again in the second stanza ordinary speech rhythm is deliberately disturbed by the line ending to give the suggestion of mounting to a pausing point and then dropping:

> Repeat a prayer also on behalf of
> Women who have seen their sons or husbands
> Setting forth, and not returning...

The third stanza brings a culmination of the long swinging movement. The end of the first line gives for the last time the choppy, interrupted effect, through the pause after 'and':

> Also pray for those who were in ships, and...

then the next three lines work up a continuously mounting swing:

> Ended their voyage on the sand, in the sea's lips
> Or in the dark throat which will not reject them
> Or wherever cannot reach them the sound of the sea bell's
> Perpetual angelus.

The inversion in the last two lines is worth noting as an indication of the importance Eliot attached to getting a long continuous upswing before the final clang of the bell. The prose order would have been 'Or wherever the sound of the sea bell's perpetual angelus cannot reach them'. A first inversion comes in order to end on the swing and hard-hitting sound of 'Perpetual angelus', but that change by itself could have given the lines

> Or wherever the sound cannot reach them of the sea bell's
> Perpetual angelus.

The first line would then have tended to split into three sense and rhythm units:

> Or wherever the sound / cannot reach them / of the sea bell's...

With the second inversion Eliot got a single clearly marked caesura,
dividing the line into a first half with a choppy, disturbed movement,
followed by a slower swing that foreshadows the broad rhythmical
pattern of the final line:

> Or wherever cannot reach them / the sound of the sea bell's
> Perpetual angelus.

I am not suggesting that the rhythmical pattern, if it were in some
way disembodied, freed from the words and their sense, could of
itself convey a recognizable sense of wave movement, but only that
it reinforces what the sense suggests.

It scarcely needs adding that such a suggestion of external movement would be no more than a virtuoso exhibition if it were not intimately appropriate to other aspects of this section of the poem.
The contrasting forms of movement it offers, the restlessness and
the steady swing, accord with the busy concerns of sea traffic and
with the necessity for acquiescence in the facts of death and mourning.

Important as the rhythmical suggestion of external movement can be,
the direct expression of states of being – states of 'mind' and 'feeling'
– through the rhythm of verse almost certainly counts for more. To
say that speech rhythm is basically a form of bodily movement is to
classify it with many other types of bodily movement that are also in
part expressive: gesture pre-eminently, but manner of walking too,
besides bigger movements of the trunk and head such as stooping
forward or holding oneself upright or sidling a little as one walks,
habits of movement which gradually produce characteristics of posture. All these form part of the group of studies which have been
elevated into an academic specialism under the term 'kinesics'.

An exaggerated statement of the relation between rhythm, in
speech and writing, and other bodily movements was to be found in
the old theory, supported for instance by Morris W. Croll, that
dancing is the source of verse rhythm. Croll's modern editor (Croll,
1966) makes the comment that 'While credible and often stated,
Prof. Croll's theory that the origin of music and verse lies in dance,
is of course pure conjecture' (p. 371). I should rather say that it is not

only conjectural but altogether improbable and quite unnecessary. Since it is impossible to speak the language without rhythmizing, and since all the varieties of rhythm occur naturally in speech, it is not difficult to suppose that verse could emerge as a selection from, and a development of, speech without any intermediary in the form of dancing, although no doubt exclamations or phrases of prayer accompanying dance movements might be effective early forms of verse.

Much more important than speculation about origins is the recognition that speech rhythm continues permanently to be part of much wider (and almost certainly much finer and unobservable) systems of bodily movement. In the early days of the English school in Cambridge Mansfield Forbes used to read Blake's 'Daybreak':

> To find the western path,
> Right through the gates of wrath
> I urge my way...

with heavy stress on each syllable of the third line and a sustained thrust on 'urge' which one felt really could carry him right through the gates of wrath. (This is a case where the sense and speech rhythm invite rather than enforce an expressive emphasis; an insensitive reading could treat the line as two iambic feet.) And James Sutherland (1934) perceives rhythmical effects as part of, or analogous to, broader systems of movement when he draws attention to the different rhythmical effect of the opening lines of Wordsworth's 'The Idiot Boy' and Coleridge's 'The Ancient Mariner':

> 'Tis eight o'clock – a clear March night –

and

> It is an ancient Mariner,

the first 'almost jaunty', the other 'almost stealthy in its subdued pounce upon the reader's attention'. As Sutherland well observes, 'To say that Wordsworth and Coleridge have both opened with a four-foot iambic line is to leave almost everything still unsaid' (pp. 79–80). An attempt must be made in the following chapter to identify the kind of thing which in such a case may have been left unsaid.

# 8

# Modes of energy release in rhythm

In poetry the chief importance of the pattern of rhythmical movement is that it forms an integral part of a total state of being. It is not
that it merely conveys and expresses states of mind and feeling; it is
part of them. This is the basis of the ancient belief that every emotion
has its own appropriate rhythm. Speaking of musical settings for
Biblical words, St Augustine wrote 'I feel that all the various emotions of the heart have rhythms proper to them in verse and song,
whereby, by some mysterious affinity, they are made more alive'
(quoted by Peter Brown, 1967). Wordsworth put the same conviction
in more general terms in the Preface to the Lyrical Ballads:

... if the Poet's words should be incommensurate with the passion, and inade-
quate to raise the Reader to a height of desirable excitement, then (unless the
Poet's choice of his metre has been grossly injudicious), in the feelings of
pleasure which the Reader has been accustomed to connect with metre in general,
and in the feeling, whether cheerful or melancholy, which he has been accustomed
to connect with that particular movement of metre, there will be found something which will greatly contribute to impart passion to the words, and to effect
the complex end which the Poet proposes to himself.

At the extremes this probably has some truth; a quick tripping or
jogging metrical form is difficult to reconcile with a mournful theme.
It may, admittedly, be used for deliberate contrast with the theme,
as Poe used it:

> Thank heaven! the crisis –
> The danger is past,
> And the lingering illness
> Is over at last –
> And the fever called 'Living'
> Is conquer'd at last.

It is questionable whether the contrast effect succeeds in the poem
as a whole, or even in the more sombre two-stress lines of Hood:

One more Unfortunate,
Weary of breath,
Rashly importunate,
Gone to her death!

And beyond question 'the Poet's choice of his metre has been grossly injudicious' in some of W. E. Henley's verse; here he describes the victim of an accident brought to hospital:

As with varnish red and glistening
Dripped his hair, his feet looked rigid;
Raised he settled stiffly sideways:
You could see his hurts were spinal.

He had fallen from an engine,
And been dragged along the metals.
It was hopeless, and they knew it;
So they covered him, and left him.

Metre like this is a superadded repellent. But whatever the truth of Wordsworth's view at the simple extremes, we should be on a wild-goose chase in looking for a match between mood and metre in the intervening range. For one thing a great diversity of rhythm is possible within the same metrical form, and moreover many qualities of speech besides the pattern of syllabic salience influence its expressive effect – as Milton showed in the *tour de force* of using the same metre for 'L'Allegro' and 'Il Penseroso'.

More plausible, if vaguer, claims can be made for a correspondence between emotion and rhythm. The antecedent processes, nebulous and fluid, from which words emerge may include those patterns of incipient movement, suggesting the rhythms, which constituted Eliot's first awareness of the gathering shape of a poem. He repeated in his lecture on Matthew Arnold his sense of the remote depths of the mind at which rhythm can operate:

What I call the 'auditory imagination' is the feeling for syllable and rhythm, penetrating far below the conscious levels of thought and feeling, invigorating every word, sinking to the most primitive and forgotten, returning to the origin and bringing something back, seeking the beginning and the end. (pp. 118–19)
(*The Use of Poetry and the Use of Criticism*)

This is more decoratively rhetorical than Eliot's best critical writing, but what it points to may be there.

By implication D. H. Lawrence as a young man said the same thing when he wrote to Edward Marsh (18 August 1913):

I think you will find my verse smoother not because I consciously attend to rhythms, but because I am no longer so criss-crossy in myself. I think, don't you know, that my rhythms fit my mood pretty well, in the verse. And if the mood is out of joint, the rhythm often is. I have always tried to get an emotion out in its own course, without altering it. It needs the finest instinct imaginable, much finer than the skill of the craftsmen...Remember skilled verse is dead in fifty years – I am thinking of your admiration of Flecker.

(*The Letters of D. H. Lawrence*)

There are two sides to any correspondence; and the question arises of the nature of the emotional states with which rhythm might accord. We are not likely nowadays to think of 'an emotion' as an entity existing by itself and distinguished sharply from the other emotions. The emotional aspect of our being is more like a spectrum of colours, a continuum named only at arbitrary points, and a spectrum of which the bands, broader or narrower, are continuously varying in brightness, with now and again exceptionally high intensity in one narrow band. In the emotional spectrum these high intensities are what we most easily identify and name – by such terms as rage, grief, delight, terror.

All the emotional states express – in fact are – our estimate and evaluation of the thing we face: we find it welcome or unwelcome in some degree; we assess it as formidable and intimidating perhaps, or highly unwelcome but vulnerable enough to be met with opposition and anger, as delightful and to be joyfully seized, quietly pleasant and to be enjoyed effortlessly, irremediable and demanding grieved resignation, or potentially disturbing but not beyond the care-discarding attitude of amusement.

Most of our time passes with the whole emotional spectrum rather dim, a pale rainbow, though with some band of allied colours predominant in brightness, according as our 'mood' is sombre, buoyant, anxious, irritable. 'Mood' describes a readiness for the time being to allow one range of allied emotions to be more easily activated than another; the corresponding fact in literature is the 'key' or 'register' in which we feel a work to be written, preparing us for one sort of emotion rather than another (and opening the way to special effects of contrast, such as comic 'relief', as it used to be called in a Shakespeare tragedy). The change from a background mood to a more sharply defined emotional response means that a somewhat narrower band of the emotional spectrum gains in intensity, but generally a band still wide enough to include a number of allied but distinguishable shades of feeling. The merging of emotional attitudes is an everyday experience: disgust may have an edging of anger or contempt, contempt may border on pity, delight and relief may go together or delight may be tinged with regret for its transience – and these are the very simplest mergings, altogether crude compared with the complex and subtle emotional colourings that the context of a poem or a play can give to the words used at a particular point.

It is impossible to believe that rhythms in themselves can make such fine discriminations as words can, in all their subtlety of sense and association. If rhythm accords with emotional colouring at all it is likely to be with a fairly wide band, not just with one point on the emotional spectrum. In this respect it is similar to other expressive movements. The postures and the patterns of movement that go with pensiveness, weariness and sadness, for example, have much in common; and the possible significance of a rhythm is likely to be equally broad. To define the state of emotion within narrower limits requires the meaning of words or a knowledge of the circumstances; the rhythm may reinforce what is defined, or at times modify it, but it will not by itself convey the precise shade of feeling. Anger, impatience, excited decision, scorn, vigorous determination, all such states of mind have something in common, and a rhythm like Dryden's

All, all of a piece throughout...

could reinforce any of them.

In mentioning weariness and vigorous determination among these states of mind I have intentionally gone beyond emotional states in the strict sense of evaluative attitudes and included terms that refer to the availability and deployment of our 'energy' (to use a term which is possibly only a metaphor but serves conveniently). It seems to me probable that, rather than according directly with particular emotional states, rhythm reflects – or, more properly, is itself part of – the energy conditions that accompany emotion. The characteristics of our imagined energy expenditure – our readiness to exert much or little of our available strength, and to exert it in specifiable ways, for instance stealthily or jauntily (as Sutherland suggested), boldly or hesitantly, restlessly, steadily – these are the features of our

total state that are likeliest to be reflected in rhythm. They are, of
course, closely bound up with emotional states: mournful sadness
usually goes with a low level of energy release and heavy, plodding
rhythms of movement; more frantic grief with impetuous or perhaps
jagged rhythms; anger with abrupt and hammering stresses; delight
with crisp, quick movement. But these are crudities of correspondence. The achievement of gifted writers is to manage infinitely
subtler shades of emotional and energy states, with delicate and
complex mergings that justify themselves by the very fact of defying
paraphrase.

The suggested deployment of energy in some specified way
commonly comes from the writer's (or his persona's) interpretation
of events, not from the events themselves. Here is Wordsworth conveying the 'perpetual whirl of trivial objects' in the life of London by
describing Bartholomew Fair:

> All moveables of wonder, from all parts,
> Are here – Albinos, painted Indians, Dwarfs,
> The Horse of knowledge, and the learned Pig,
> The Stone-eater, the man that swallows fire,
> Giants, Ventriloquists, the Invisible Girl,
> The Bust that speaks and moves its goggling eyes,
> The Wax-work, Clock-work, all the marvellous craft
> Of modern Merlins, Wild Beasts, Puppet-shows,
> All out-o'-the-way, far-fetched, perverted things,
> All freaks of nature, all Promethean thoughts
> Of man, his dulness, madness, and their feats
> All jumbled up together, to compose
> A Parliament of Monsters. Tents and Booths
> Meanwhile, as if the whole were one vast mill,
> Are vomiting, receiving on all sides,
> Men, Women, three-years' Children, Babes in arms.
>
> (*The Prelude*, Book VII)

It comes as a surprise, on looking back at a passage that so effectively
suggests the 'perpetual whirl', to notice that it scarcely describes
movement at all; it describes a medley of trivialities, but the sense of
restlessness comes from the rhythm of the lines and the grammatical
structure.

This is one form of energy discharge. Contrast the lines in which
Wordsworth describes his scarcely conscious brooding preoccupa-
tions after the huge peak had seemed to pursue him for his boyish
offence, where the sombre, sobered mood is accompanied by a sug-

gestion of retarded activity which the rhythm certainly helps to suggest:

> No familiar shapes
> Remained, no pleasant images of trees,
> Of sea or sky, no colours of green fields;
> But huge and mighty forms, that do not live
> Like living men, moved slowly through the mind
> By day, and were a trouble to my dreams.
> (*The Prelude*, Book I)

And yet in many passages how uncertain and tentative our estimation of the effects of rhythm must be. In the lines

> With resignation, at my feet I saw
> Lake, islands, promontories, gloomy bays...

is it possible to say with complete confidence that the rhythm is inappropriate? When we substitute what Wordsworth really wrote –

> With exultation, at my feet I saw
> Lake, islands, promontories, gleaming bays...
> (*The Prelude*, Book IV)

the movement of the second line *seems* much more fitting to the vigorous delight; but the uncertainty is there, and this may be a case where the meaning of words – especially key words – alters what we read into the rhythm.

Yet there are undoubtedly passages providing the negative case, where the rhythm fails to reinforce what the words suggest. When Shelley describes the chariot of the Hours in *Prometheus Unbound* the words tell of the wild rush of speed, but they remain merely descriptive, the rhythm, though innocuous, contributing scarcely anything to the effect, unless possibly in the last four lines:

> The rocks are cloven, and through the purple night
> I see cars drawn by rainbow-wingèd steeds
> Which trample the dim winds: in each there stands
> A wild-eyed charioteer urging their flight.
> Some look behind, as fiends pursued them there,
> And yet I see no shapes but the keen stars:
> Others, with burning eyes, lean forth, and drink
> With eager lips the wind of their own speed,
> As if the thing they loved fled on before,
> And now, even now, they clasped it. Their bright locks
> Stream like a comet's flashing hair: they all
> Sweep onward.

It may be the undistinguished rhythm of some of Shelley's verse that gives the too frequent impression of an attempt to enforce emotion by describing it, instead of evoking it. Yet in 'Ozymandias' there could hardly be a better rhythmical effect than the steady continuity of the last three lines:

> 'My name is Ozymandias, king of kings:
> Look on my works, ye Mighty, and despair!'
> Nothing beside remains. Round the decay
> Of that colossal wreck, boundless and bare
> The lone and level sands stretch far away.

It is not the movement described but the movement of the verse which is the essential thing in presenting the mode of energy expenditure that the reader is invited to enter into. Two contrasting stanzas of 'The Ancient Mariner' show the rhythmical patterning of the words contributing as much as their sense, or more. The first gives the impression of melodramatic suddenness in what happens when the last throw of the dice decides the Mariner's fate:

> The Sun's rim dips; the stars rush out:
> At one stride comes the dark;
> With far-heard whisper, o'er the sea,
> Off shot the spectre-bark.

The short rhythmical units, clearly defined by pauses of sense and punctuation, and the sharp blows of many adjacent heavy stresses, reinforce the sense of decisiveness. (In a different context the same rhythms could accord with a peremptory attitude.) In contrast, consider the smooth continuity, with nearly all the rhythm units flowing one into the next, of the stanza coming after the nadir of the Mariner's suffering, when he is ready to emerge from his worst self-hatred and rediscover the possibility of feeling love:

> The moving Moon went up the sky,
> And nowhere did abide:
> Softly she was going up,
> And a star or two beside –

The rhythms emerge from the state of mind, especially from the nature of the movement and energy discharge it is attuned to; and it is through this that the external movement is interpreted.

Of course only a small proportion of rhythmically expressive lines make any reference to movement; their own syllabic movement is what counts. And even when other movement is mentioned it need not be imitated. It is the very delicate half-suggestion of the natural movement that contributes to the deep effect of Henry King's lines:

> But heark! My Pulse like a soft Drum
> Beats my approach, tells *Thee* I come...

A still further hint of the bodily movement, this time of breathing, probably comes into our understanding of Hamlet's lines as he dies:

> And in this harsh world draw thy breath in pain,
> To tell my story...

When it comes to lines whose own rhythmical movement is expressive, without any suggestion of other activity, the most readily identified type is one in which perturbation of mind and emotional disorganization are conveyed through interruptions in a flowing rhythm or disturbances in an established rhythmical set. One form of this device, simple, perhaps over-contrived, occurs in *The Merchant of Venice* when Portia is confessing to Bassanio, before he has made choice of the caskets, that she has fallen in love with him:

> Beshrew your eyes!
> They have o'erlook'd me and divided me:
> One half is yours, the other half yours –
> Mine own, I would say, but if mine, then yours...

where the stumble of sense – 'yours' for 'mine own' – is made to produce a stumble in the regular metre as well. A subtler and more serious use of the same device occurs in *Hamlet* when Claudius makes his desperate attempt at penitent prayer:

> Try what repentance can: what can it not?
> Yet what can it when one can not repent?    (III, iii, 65–6)

Uncertainty about the position of the stresses in the second line adds to the confusedness of the utterance and the sense of bafflement; none of the possible speech rhythms will let the second line flow like the first.

Of *Macbeth* it has been suggested that the disturbance of right order (a major theme of the play, as L. C. Knights has argued) is emphasized by the frequently abrupt and disjointed rhythms. There is a telling contrast, rhythmically, between Macduff's outcry when he rushes in, shocked, to report Duncan's murder and a speech with similar emotional colouring in Dryden's *All for Love*, both nominally

in iambic pentameters. Serapion has to announce the defection of
Cleopatra's fleet to the Romans:

> *Alexas.*    How frightfully the holy coward stares
> As if not yet recovered of the assault,
> When all his gods, and, what's more dear to him,
> His offerings, were at stake.
> *Serapion.*                    O horror, horror!
> Egypt has been; our latest hour has come...

Dryden disturbs the steady beat –

> His offerings were at stake. O horror, horror! –

too little to enforce rhythmically the irruption of emotion that the
sense of Serapion's words presents. Shakespeare disrupts the smooth
flow more expressively; the talk has been of the rough night:

> *Lennox.*    My young remembrance cannot parallel
> A fellow to it.
> *Macduff.*                   O horror! horror! horror!
> Tongue nor heart cannot conceive, nor name thee!

The effect comes not just from the triple 'horror' but from the extra
syllables in the line divided between the two speakers and from the
complex rhythms of the following line where, instead of Dryden's
simple caesura, there are two sharp breaks, one after 'heart', the
other after 'conceive' (where the comma insists on a pause which
might not otherwise be made).

The expressive value of disturbed rhythms is well brought out by
Southall (1964). He notes one of the rare occasions when Sidney
departs from his rather facile smoothness:

> I might! – unhappie word – Once, I might,
> And then would not, or could not, see my blisse;
> Till now wrapt in a most infernall night,
> I find how heavenly day, wretch! I did misse.

Southall comments

The easy Elizabethan facility is replaced by the hesitant, pausing rhythms of
Wyatt, something close to the perplexed freedom of Shakespeare and the intrica-
cies of Donne. But perhaps even more immediately than Donne and Shakespeare,
Sidney's lines bring to mind Hopkins. This is probably due to the recollection of

> Here! creep
> Wretch, under a comfort serves in a whirlwind

prompted by Sidney's fourth line. But the connection with Hopkins is deeper
than that suggested by the parenthetic self-castigation of 'wretch' and lies in the
disturbed, uneasy rhythms. (p. 156)

And Southall, echoing Knights's phrase about Macbeth's line, points to the see-sawing of the rhythm in many of Wyatt's lines; for example:

> It may be good like it who list
> but I do doubt who can me blame
> for oft assured yet have I myst
> and now again I fere the same.

He goes on

The effect of pairing off phrases in this way is to create just such a see-sawing movement, emulating the pitch and toss of the divided mind, the uncertainties and hesitations with which Wyatt's figures are hedged about. It is in such a way that when, in the Psalms, David, pondering the Christian mysteries, pulls himself up short,

> as who myght say . who hathe exprest this thing?
> I synner I / what have I sayd alas?

the perplexity of David is realized in the rhythm of the lines. (p. 147)

Catherine Ing (1951) puts it in general terms when she says 'Statements may come with different emotional force according to whether they are made smoothly and plainly or hesitatingly and with struggle'.

In speaking of emotional *force* she tacitly refers to the characteristics of energy expenditure which I take to be the essential expressive feature of rhythm. It is not just 'forcefulness' in the ordinary sense which is in question. A slowed, or hesitating, or tentative movement may be the outcome of great inner energy and rhythmical control, and totally different from flaccidity, whether in mechanical regularity or slack formlessness. The slow movement of Wordsworth's lines about the 'huge and mighty forms, that do not live Like living men' is one form of intense activity, brooding and inward-turned. A different kind of retarded, pensive movement, but at its best still firmly organized, accompanies the unemphatic sadness of some of Edward Thomas's poems:

> For had I health I could not ride or run or fly
> So far or so rapidly over the land
> As I desire: I should reach Wiltshire tired;
> I should have changed my mind before I could be in Wales.
> I could not love; I could not command love.
>                                    ('Health')

or his restrained touch as he handles an experience to discover what it was:

> 'In my memory
> Again and again I see it, strangely dark,
> And vacant of a life but just withdrawn.
> We have not seen the woodman with the axe.
> Some ghost has left it now as we two came.'
> 'And yet you doubted if this were the road?'
> 'Well, sometimes I have thought of it and failed
> To place it. No. And I am not quite sure,
> Even now, this is it. For another place,
> Real or painted, may have combined with it.
> Or I myself a long way back in time...'
>                          ('The Chalk-Pit')

The rhythmical unity of the line

> To place it. No. And I am not quite sure,

criss-crossing with natural speech phrases, illustrates the command he could exercise in the act of seeming tentative and uncertain.

It is an entirely different deployment of energy that characterizes many of Donne's rhythms, the vehemence for instance of

> Batter my heart, three-personed God...

or the vigour fused with irritable protest in the line

> For God's sake hold your tongue, and let me love...

Contrasting with these forms of movement Donne could offer the slowed, weighed-down progress of a penitent's line, after speaking of the bodies awaiting the Resurrection:

> But let them sleep, Lord, and me mourn a space...

or the unemphatic, everyday flow, with scarcely a caesura, of the first part of the line

> What if this present were...

followed by the awed slowing of the final syllables

> ...the world's last night?

The mode of releasing energy revealed even in single lines may be still more evident in longer passages. The pent-up annoyance, expressed spasmodically at first and then rising into spate, as Brutus and Cassius quarrel, is conveyed by the rhythmical structure as well as the sense of the passage:

*Cassius.*   Urge me no more, I shall forget myself;
Have mind upon your health, tempt me no further.
*Marcus Brutus.*   Away, slight man!
*Cassius.*   Is't possible?
*Marcus Brutus.*                              Hear me, for I will speak.
Must I give way and room to your rash choler?
Shall I be frighted when a madman stares?
*Cassius.*   O ye gods, ye gods! must I endure all this?
*Marcus Brutus.*   All this! ay, more: fret till your proud heart break;
Go show your slaves how choleric you are,
And make your bondmen tremble. Must I budge?
Must I observe you? must I stand and crouch
Under your testy humour? By the gods,
You shall digest the venom of your spleen,
Though it do split you; for, from this day forth,
I'll use you for my mirth, yea, for my laughter,
When you are waspish.

The release of pent-up force in cumulative rhythms – like more and more uninhibited gestures – may be associated with entirely different emotion. Instead of Brutus's anger, here is Claudio's terror in *Measure for Measure*:

Ay, but to die, and go we know not where;
To lie in cold obstruction, and to rot;
This sensible warm motion to become
A kneaded clod; and the delighted spirit
To bathe in fiery floods, or to reside
In thrilling region of thick-ribbed ice;
To be imprison'd in the viewless winds,
And blown with restless violence round about
The pendent world; or to be worse than worst
Of those that lawless and incertain thought
Imagine howling! – 'tis too horrible!

The two passages differ in their component rhythms – the short units like repeated blows from Brutus, Claudio's longer shudderings - but the torrent of energy unites them.

Instead of the rhetoric of the cumulative rhythmical passage another poet will secure ironic effects through a deliberate jerkiness, with parentheses and interjections to check the forward flow of movement, as Ezra Pound does:

For two hours he talked of Gallifet;
Of Dowson; of the Rhymers' Club;
Told me how Johnson (Lionel) died
By falling from a high stool in a pub...

> But showed no trace of alcohol
> At the autopsy, privately performed –
> Tissue preserved – the pure mind
> Arose toward Newman as the whisky warmed.
>
> ('Siena mi fe; disfecemi Maremma')

A check and change in the pattern of movement serves Hardy to suggest the broken state of bereavement in the poem that begins 'Woman much missed, how you call to me, call to me':

> Or is it only the breeze, in its listlessness
> Travelling across the wet mead to me here,
> You being ever dissolved to wan wistlessness,
> Heard no more again far or near?
>
> Thus I; faltering forward,
> Leaves around me falling,
> Wind oozing thin through the thorn from norward,
> And the woman calling.
>
> ('The Voice')

Just as there are innumerable ways of mobilizing, withholding and releasing our energy, so the movement of verse has an indefinite range of resources for suggesting these possibilities. Dryden secures a contemptuous, almost spitting emphasis on 'politicks' in the lines

> Chastiz'd, he ought to have retreated Home,
> But He reads politicks to *Absolom*.

The effect depends largely on the slowing down produced by the two adjacent stresses 'Hé réads' (helped by the capital for 'He'), from which one is launched into the plosive initial sound of the key word.

The effect of momentary poising and launching is gained above all by the pivoting from one line to the next, where there need be no break in the sound but only a prolongation of one consonant before it turns into the next:

> . . . like a soft Drum
> Beats my approach . . .

The launching from the line's end may give special force not simply to the first word of the next line but to a whole phrase; so Duncan, as Macbeth makes his entry:

> He was a Gentleman on whom I built
> An absolute trust.

But very often it is the first word of the following line that receives special emphasis. In one of Herrick's poems, 'To Perilla', he anticipates his death and gives her instructions for various rituals of mourning, and the poem ends

> Then lastly, let some weekly-strewings be
> Devoted to the memory of me:
> Then shall my Ghost not walk about, but keep
> Still in the coole, and silent shades of sleep.

The emphasis on 'Still' helps to bring out the double meaning of 'keep still' – remain immobile, and also abide always, for ever, in the shades.

In less regular verse the point at which lines of variable length are ended can produce even more decisive effects. It would tremendously weaken the force of Eliot's lines in 'Marina' to alter the position of the line ending to:

> Those who sharpen the tooth of the dog,
> Meaning death

instead of

> Those who sharpen the tooth of the dog, meaning
> Death
> Those who glitter with the glory of the hummingbird, meaning
> Death

and so on. Eliot had extraordinary command of what could be done with the break between lines. Take for example an imperative statement in prose, 'But set down this, set down this'; it has considered force and emphasis with its succession of stressed syllables, but nothing like the combined emphasis and reflectiveness and finality that Eliot produces by abandoning the prose punctuation in favour of line endings:

>                          . . . but set down
> This set down
> This: . . .
>                              ('Journey of the Magi')

The expressive value of the line ending depends largely on the fact of its defining rhythmical sub-units that would otherwise merge in a continuous flow. Thus in the prose phrase, 'so long as nature will bear up with this exercise', the word 'will' can fuse rhythmically with both the preceding and the following units, which therefore

flow together, each losing its distinct character: 'so long as nature
will' and 'will bear up'. But the line ending creates two units:

> ...So long as nature
> Will bear up with this exercise...
>
> (*The Winter's Tale*, III, ii)

Earlier in the same speech Leontes' decision, printed as prose, would
most naturally be phrased 'upon them / shall the causes of their
deaths appear / unto our shame perpetual'. The line endings create
different rhythmical units:

> ...upon them shall
> The causes of their deaths appear, unto
> Our shame perpetual...

giving much stronger weight to 'The causes' and 'Our shame'.

Another potentially expressive feature of a rhythmical movement,
long or short, is the way it ends. The fitness of rhythm in Eliot's line
about the way the world ends,

> Not with a bang but a whimper

would be lost without the weak stress at the end –

> With a whimper not with a bang.

He had great mastery of the rhythms that shade off into silence:

> What seas what shores what granite islands towards my timbers
> And woodthrush calling through the fog
> My daughter.
>
> ('Marina')

Contrast with that the snapping off, the finality of contempt and
disgust, in Pope's lines:

> His daughter flaunts a viscount's tawdry wife;
> She bears a coronet, and pox, for life.
>
> ('Moral Essays: Epistle III')

An altogether different conclusiveness, a boldly rhetorical rounding
off, closes Yeats's 'Byzantium':

> Marbles of the dancing floor
> Break bitter furies of complexity,
> Those images that yet
> Fresh images beget,
> That dolphin-torn, that gong-tormented sea.

But the possibilities of rhythmical movement are innumerable, and their effects are part of the literary critic's concern, and any reader's concern, with particular works; and – it scarcely needs saying – the rhythm has always to be viewed in relation with all the other factors at work. The purpose of an abstract discussion is to clarify the nature of rhythm and to see as far as possible what effects it can reasonably be supposed to have and what kind of relation with other elements in a poem, especially with sense and with the features of tempo, intonation and qualities of voice that the sense suggests as appropriate. We might want to consider, for example, two further passages by Yeats, in which there are many similarities of rhythm but a sharply different emotional effect. One comes in 'Vacillation, V' after the line

> Responsibility so weighs me down.
>
> Things said or done long years ago,
> Or things I did not do or say
> But thought that I might say or do,
> Weigh me down, and not a day
> But something is recalled,
> My conscience or my vanity appalled.

The other comes at the end of 'A Dialogue of Self and Soul':

> When such as I cast out remorse
> So great a sweetness flows into the breast
> We must laugh and we must sing,
> We are blest by everything,
> Everything we look upon is blest.

Look at the similarity in rhythm between

> Weigh me down, and not a day

and

> We must laugh and we must sing...

Admittedly there is a rhythmical difference: 'Weigh me down,', with its comma and its echo of the earlier phrase, is held apart from the following phrase; there can be none of the excited hurry of 'We must laugh and we must sing'. But intonation comes in too: 'Buoys me up, and not a day', with its rise of pitch on 'up', has nothing of the same emotional quality. Scansion misses everything; it would be the same, apart from the initial light stress, for

My conscience or my vanity appalled

as for

Everything we look upon is blest.

The light and rapid syllables of the second of the lines decisively alter the rhythmical movement. Yet there still are rhythmical similarities in the two passages: each, even the first, has a vigour and decisiveness that present a sharp contrast with, say, the tentative, emotionally exploratory, rhythms of Edward Thomas already quoted. Like the other forms of expressive bodily movement – gesture, gait and so on – characteristic rhythms distinguish one writer from another.

Admittedly, like those other patterns of movement, rhythm becomes to some extent conventionalized in its expressive significance; just as the shrug, the bow or the smile has a more or less agreed meaning in a given culture, so we have the conventional tripping measures or mournful numbers in verse. But more intrinsically, and independently of convention, our expressive movements, including our speech rhythms, reflect levels of energy and the ways in which it is being deployed – smoothly and steadily, restlessly, hesitantly, explosively, with strong determination, with cumulative force. Expressive changes can take place while a sequence of rhythms unfolds: they may be changes from the smooth to the abrupt, from the flowing to the broken, accelerations and slowings, variations between clarity of rhythmical outline and doubtful or minimally marked patterning.

In a further respect, too, the rhythms of speech are like the other bodily movement systems of everyday life: they are for the most part *not* expressive – they are emotionally and energically neutral. It could hardly be otherwise. A great part of the communication and exploration for which language is used demands that emotion should be held in check, its expression damped down or postponed, while more exact descriptions, definitions, statements of problems, extended arguments or instructions are being attempted. Fine poetry succeeds in conveying its perceptual discriminations and exact shades of meaning without having to diminish emotion; and expressive rhythm is one of its vital means to that end. The vapidity of some of the connective tissue in *The Prelude*, for instance, is partly due to its rhythmical inertness, or the rhythmical flatness is one evidence that no pressure of emotion was fused with the thinking. It is tempting to call the lifeless passages prosy, but that would be misleading if it implied that prose can safely disregard its rhythmical organization. The rhythms of prose raise special questions which it is time to examine.

# 9

# Rhythms in prose

The assumption that rhythm was somehow bound up essentially with regularity and repetition, with metrical feet and scansion, was an unpromising start for any understanding of the rhythms of prose. It led in the wrong direction. Something measurable or countable was sought out, something to bring prose within range of the labelling operations which gave reassurance to the scholar confronting poetry.

Even the attempt to establish isochronous intervals as the basis of rhythm in verse, which I described as a will-o'-the-wisp pursuit, spread, rather oddly, into the study of prose rhythm, most painstakingly and objectively in the work of André Classe (1939). He puts forward the vague statement that rhythm is experienced when the divisions of a sentence 'have particular relative durations', but with no indication what 'particular' may mean here. In ordinary conversations, he says, 'stresses occur at intervals which vary considerably, but only exceptionally become either very large or very small... And the more rhythmical the speech is, the more regular the intervals seem to become, if we may trust to impressions' (p. 50). The argument is fatally circular: how does he know that some speech is 'more rhythmical'? – only through the impression that the stresses are coming at regular intervals; and this he then claims to discover as the mark of rhythmical speech. He has defined his term 'rhythm' in such a way as to make his hypothesis a truism.

But with objective measurement he entirely failed to find what he was loooking for in prose. He measured the way readers distributed their time over successive sections of sentences, and he consistently failed to find evidence that English sentences are divided into sections or 'bars' of equal duration. The test, he writes, 'provides no evidence that the hypothesis of isochronism is valid for prose' (p. 57). The strange thing – evidence of the pertinacity with which a preconception may be clung to – is that Classe then labours almost pathetically to save something of the hypothesis; he writes, for instance, that 'isochronism often means nothing more than a sort of ideal which may be frequently realized, but more often is not, especially when the rhythmic tendency has to contend with other factors which obscure its effects...' The quite simple fact is that Classe usefully put to objective test the belief that prose is divided up into isochronous units, and his results refuted it.

The conviction of there being a tendency to isochronism in both speech and prose has been held by such eminent writers that one hesitates to put it aside. It may be noted in passing that if it could be established as a fact for speech and prose it would no longer serve those other writers who want to make it the distinguishing mark of verse. As far as speech and prose are concerned there is presumably a grain of truth in the notion of equal time intervals between stresses, a very small grain. This is that a succession of lightly stressed syllables between two strong stresses is taken slightly faster the longer it is. Consider this series of phrases: push harder; push it harder; push it a bit harder; push it a little bit harder. Although the interval between the heavily stressed syllables 'push' and 'hard' does get progressively longer it doesn't increase in proportion to the number of intervening light syllables. The phoneticians (for example Pike and Abercrombie) are agreed on this, but they have to express it very cautiously. Pike (1945) writes that in English prose 'The units [of rhythm] *tend* to follow one another in such a way that the lapse of time between the beginning of their prominent syllables is *somewhat* uniform' (my italics) (p. 34). Abercrombie (1965) is similarly cautious, though both these writers then go on to make more of this approximate isochronism than to my mind can be justified. The slight phonetic tendency is far too slender a foundation for the superstructure that Classe hoped to erect upon it.

Why, in any event, isochronous intervals should have any merit or any particular effect is never explained. Nor is it easy to decide whether some passages of prose are lacking in isochronism, either managing to avoid it or failing to achieve it; we are offered no examples. And it is difficult to guess in what way, if there were such passages, they would suffer by the lack; one could equally well expect them to be less boring.

Literary scholars, of whom Saintsbury (1912) was representative, expressed themselves more subjectively and impressionistically. They conveyed emphatic literary judgements, but their analyses achieved little; in fact it is sometimes uncertain what their purpose was and what questions they thought it worth while asking. Saintsbury analysed prose along the lines of the prosody he employed for metrical verse. His massive *History of English Prose Rhythm* is still an impressive monument to his range of reading, and it provides in effect an anthology of prose writing in English, with a commentary that reflects the prejudices and preferences of the unshakeably assured academic of the late nineteenth century. Within the limits of his range of enjoyment much of what he says springs from closely attentive appreciation and is still helpful, though the style makes it uncongenial reading today with its mannered sentence structure, its orotundities of vocabulary, and its ponderous humour – the style whose vestiges survived until recently in the orations with which recipients of honorary degrees were hailed.

When he attempts general statements about prose rhythm Saintsbury is so vague as to elucidate nothing. He speaks of 'that undulating movement, balanced but varied, parallel but not stichic, which constitutes the rhythm of prose' (p. 51). Paraphrased, this says that in prose there are no successive lines of the same metrical form, but there are sections of the utterance that are 'balanced' against one another. This may refer to phrases of about the same length, or perhaps similar in their pattern of stressed and lightly stressed syllables, or – possibly – similar in syntactic structure. The sections of the movement are 'parallel'; and this too may refer to their syntactic form, or it may be no more than an equally vague way of saying that they have 'balance'. These things, whatever they are precisely, form part of a wavelike movement – which suggests runs of syllables building up to a main stress or pause, followed by a broadly similar but not identical pattern. We should have to add that patterns of pitch change, as well as stress differences, form part of the total effect. In a metaphorical way Saintsbury has given a vague indication of what we all perceive in some kinds of prose.

In discussing Hooker, for instance, he speaks of his 'adaptation of the periodic *structure* of the classical sentence to a larger periodic *rhythm*; the abrupter and more intrusive parallelism or balance, as we find it in Lyly and others, being widened, softened, and moulded out into great undulating sweeps of phrase, rising, hovering, descending, with a wing-like motion' (p. 136). Saintsbury does this sort of thing well; he has a sensitive perception of what distinguishes a writer, and he draws attention to what deserves attention and what might be the subject of much more precisely formulated description or analysis if we knew how to set about it.

His own further analysis consists almost entirely of notating samples of prose as if they were verse except for the lines. He divides it with bar lines into feet, and in selected sections he indicates the stressed and unstressed syllables (though he regards these (p. 341) as 'long' and 'short'). An example is his treatment (pp. 161–2) of a passage by Fulke Greville:

Again, / if it be true / which the philo / sophers hold, / that virtues / and vices, / disagreeing / in all things / else, / yet agree / in this, / that where / there is one / *in posse*, / *in esse* / there are all, / then cannot / any excellent / faculty / of the mind / be alone, / but it must needs / have wisdom, / patience, / piety, / and all other / enemies / of chance / to accompany it, / ăs ăgāinst / ănd ămōngst / āll stōrms / ă cālmed / ănd cālmĭng / *mēns* / *ădēptă*.

It is not at all clear what Saintsbury thought he had achieved by his scansion. Its most useful purpose would have been to indicate how he believed the passage should be read, and at many points in the book this is clearly what he claims for it. Yet here, and elsewhere, this intention is balked by another, that of superimposing on the actual rhythms of reading a scheme of notional 'feet' derived from metrical theory; although he has described prose rhythm as lacking the lines and repeated patterns of metrical writing he apparently believed that its 'balanced' or 'parallel' undulations should be metrically scanned. In the passage from Greville some of the feet do correspond with units of speaking or reading and the divisions fit the natural pauses:

> have wisdom, / patience, / piety, /
> all storms / a calmed / and calming / *mens* / *adepta* /

but at other points the foot divisions could never correspond with natural speaking pauses:

which the / philo / sophers hold, /
disagreeing / in all things / else, /
then cannot / any excellent / faculty / of the mind / be alone, /

It cannot be said that this kind of exercise draws attention to structural balance in the sound of the passage, or to parallel sections; it seems to serve no purpose at all.

Saintsbury is nowhere explicit about the principles by which he decides which syllables should be taken together to form a foot. He merely lists the classical varieties of metrical feet and then divides prose into them in what seems for much of the time an arbitrary way. His scansion only occasionally indicates a choice between two possible ways of reading, and at these points what he offers is simply a notation of a reading that he has decided on without the aid of prosody. He does at one point (p. 345) refer to 'The foot-division, inseparable from rhythm and scarcely capable of extension beyond the fifth syllable...', implying that one main stress can serve as the salient element in a rhythm unit made up of five syllables but usually not more. It is probably true that beyond that number we shall subdivide the syllables with a second stress. Apart from this he indicates no principle that could determine the foot division; he is left only with his judgement of the best phrasing, and this turns the scansion merely into a notation of what he has chosen on other grounds.

Thus, for instance, he claimed to demonstrate the importance of the foot division by his scansion of a phrase of Swinburne's prose:

Frŏm hĕr stāinlĕss / ănd Ŏlȳmpĭăn / sūmmĭt, / ŏf dĭvīne / ĭndĭffĕrĕnt / līght...

He suggests that without the word 'and' it could be taken as two lines of verse and scanned differently:

From her stain / less Olym / pian sum / mit
Of divine, / indif / ferent light...

Of this second line he says 'Of course, the singular persons who ask plaintively, "How a difference in naming the feet can alter the rhythm?" may see no alternative here. But to me a spondee or iamb followed and preceded by an anapaest, and an anapaest and paeon followed by a monosyllable, produce rhythms as different as a hawk from a hand-saw.' (pp. 434–5) His reply to the singular persons ignores their valid challenge. What he has done by omitting 'and' is of course to change the speech rhythms; and this is apparent to anyone who speaks English, even an ignoramus who might not recognize a paeon. The naming of the feet is redundant labelling.

Saintsbury's faint doubts, evidently reflecting criticism he had met with, are similarly expressed and similarly countered when he scans a passage from Sir William Temple:

Whĕn āll / ĭs dōne, / hūmăn / lĭfe / ĭs, / ăt thĕ grēatĕst / ănd thĕ bēst, / bŭt līke / ă frōwărd / chīld / thăt mŭst bĕ plāyed wĭth / ănd hūmŏured / ă lĭttlĕ / tŏ kēep ĭt / quĭĕt / tĭll ĭt fālls / ăslēep; / ănd thēn / thĕ cāre / ĭs ōvĕr.

He notes that 'the last half-dozen or even the last dozen words' could be given 'a continuous trochaic scansion':

and / thēn thĕ / cāre ĭs / ōvĕr.

He goes on 'To my mind and ear this would spoil the beauty of the passage; but that may be a matter of taste. What is important is the unquestionable and remarkable *difference* which these various foot-scansions make. It is surely impossible, in the face of such an example, to regard them as mere pedantic trifling' (p. 237). But here too the rival scansions simply indicate two different patterns of speech runs with their very slight pauses. We choose between them not because of anything the scansion does but in the light of our feeling for the mood of the passage and the expressive value of the optional rhythms. Saintsbury's assumption that scansion guides reading, that principles of prosody are in some way directive or pre-scriptive, is totally unfounded.

Saintsbury gives his attention mainly to the more rhetorical prose, what he calls ornate or highly rhythmed prose, and then chiefly to its more emotive passages. A similar choice is made by Morris Croll (1919), who selected for study the recurrent cadences found in the Book of Common Prayer, especially in the collects – such phrases as 'help and defend us', 'governed and sanctified', 'punished for our offences', 'in the midst of so many and great dangers'. He thought these cadences were greatly influenced by, perhaps actually derived from, varieties of clausulae in Latin oratory. He conceded that they followed a much less regular metrical pattern, but he found it worth while – for unspecified reasons – to classify them and label them according to the form of Latin cadence they most nearly approxi-mated.

Although in his analysis of verse Croll believed in isochronous intervals they played no part in his account of these prose cadences, where he was content simply to identify the pattern of stressed and unstressed syllables. He began with an identification of rhythmical groupings that was better controlled than Saintsbury's because it was anchored to a fixed point – the end of a period or of a major division within it. He indicated the stress pattern of the cadence by counting *back* from its ending and noting the number of each syllable on which a stress falls; thus (p. 304ff)

5          2
help and defend us    (planus, type 1)

6          2
supplication of thy people    (planus, type 2)

7          3
acknowledging our wretchedness    (English modification of tardus)

8          5     3
defend us from all adversities    (English modification of velox)

He allows himself a great deal of freedom by accepting minor variants within the longer patterns. Velox, for instance, includes not only 8–5–3, as above, but 9–5–3 and 8–4–2:

9          5     3
return into the way of righteousness

8          4     2
the weakness of our mortal nature.

And with longer patterns, supposedly corresponding to the trispondaic cursus, he becomes unconvincing through his arbitrary choice of stress; for instance,

9          6      4     2
such good things as pass man's understanding,

where legitimate readings might include stresses on 'things' and 'man's'.

In two further ways he gives himself yet more freedom of manoeuvre. Whereas previous writers had identified the recurrent cadences only in terminal positions – at the end of periods or at the end of divisions within a period – he showed that they might occur in intermediate positions as well. As instances he quotes 'thy bountiful goodness', 'almighty and everlasting', 'free from all adversities'. Secondly he showed (p. 340) that two different cadences might overlap, the final syllables of the first being at the same time the opening syllables of the second; for instance,

                                7              4        2 (velox)
                        5      2 (planus)
That all things may be so ordered and settled by their endeavours;

or (from Gibbon)

The successors of St. Peter and Constantine were invested
    11              7                    2 (velox)
    7                    3 (tardus)
with the purple and prerogatives of the Caesars;

or (again from Gibbon)

                          5              2 (planus)
    8              4      2 (velox)
The object of her own amazement and terror.

Croll was content with such loose approximations in English to the
strict form of the Latin clauses that he largely dissolved the fixed
character of the rhythm groups which he began by claiming. And
when he adds the further flexibility of these overlapping cadences it
becomes hard to see that he does much more than exemplify the way
in which all the continuous runs and flowings of prose are brought
about. Although repeated and familiar forms of cadence do occur,
especially in liturgical prose, there is something artificial about iso-
lating them whenever they can be detected in an ordinary prose
continuum. Still, Croll's approach did promise, and in part attain, a
more securely based method than Saintsbury's for identifying some
of the distinguishable units of prose rhythm.

Both he and Saintsbury in their different ways are picking out the
more emotive plums from the pudding. They explicitly concentrate
on prose that is closely allied to oratory, and within that they give
most attention to the more prominently patterned parts of the total
texture. This raises the question whether in ordinary prose the
rhythmical organization of the words is worth attending to at all –
whether through rhythm we gain anything that their simple sense
would not have given us. Part of the answer that Saintsbury implies
is that rhythm has an independent value in its beauty, in the diversified wholeness of its patterns of sound and movement. As I. A.
Richards (1929) showed, in his nonsense-word equivalent of a
stanza of 'On the Morning of Christ's Nativity', sound and movement in meaningless oral articulation make little appeal; but this is
not really a demonstration that they add nothing to the appeal of
meaningful material. We might say the same about colour in a painting; we could, after all, display blobs and patches of pink and red,
circles of blue, crescents and clouds of brown, in an arrangement that
made no recognizable shape and had no attraction in themselves,

but this would not mean that as colours of cheeks, lips, eyes and so on they contribute nothing to the appeal of a face. In, say, a colour photograph they can enhance and particularize the appeal of features that are perceived in other ways as well. The rhythm of meaningful prose may do the same.

This would presumably have been Saintsbury's claim when he spoke of Hooker's 'great undulating sweeps of phrase, rising, hovering, descending, with a wing-like motion'. This feature brings nothing peculiarly appropriate to a discussion of the laws of ecclesiastical polity, but what it offers would have been a welcome enhancement of pleasure in almost any treatise Hooker had undertaken. Certainly this 'aesthetic' enhancement appears to be what Saintsbury found lacking in the 'utilitarian' prose that at best held no interest for him. A similar beauty or elegance of a rather general kind is probably what Croll would have claimed to find – had he thought it necessary to say what he was looking for – in the cadences he analysed. In general they are not peculiarly appropriate to the sense of the phrases that embody them in the prayers and collects, but they are pleasing patterns of sound and movement, and as elements of a familiar liturgical idiom they move with acceptable smoothness through the mind of the worshipper.

Yet the 'aesthetic' attraction of rhythm, its appeal purely as a perceptual pattern, cannot be the whole story for a critic like Saintsbury. Here and there he is undoubtedly looking for something more, not a general beauty of phrase, but some special fitness of a particular rhythm to the mood or tone being conveyed. He says for example (p. 242) that the iambics that English runs to may be too 'solemn' when the subject is unimportant; hence the value of Addison's sometimes ending a sentence with a preposition, e.g. '...which the prophet took a distinct view of'. Similarly, when he says that to read Temple's phrase in trochaic scansion – and / thēn the / cāre is / ōver – 'would spoil the beauty of the passage', he almost certainly has in mind some fitness of the preferable rhythm to the feeling of regretful rest in the finality of death. Explicitly, in discussing Sir Thomas Browne's prose, he speaks (p. 192) of 'the unerring adjustment of the different rhythms to the different senses'. He instances the contrasting closes of three paragraphs at the end of *Garden of Cyrus*: 'the sarcastic liveliness of "the ghost of a rose"; the splendour...of "according / to the ordainer / of order / and mystical / mathematics / of the city / of heaven"; the solemnity of *a* sounds, and the arrangement of monosyllable, anapaest, and iamb, in "all / shall awake / again".' And referring to Burton's *Anatomy of Melancholy* he writes (p. 167): 'The rhythm more than suits, it positively heightens, the sense in "those fair buildings and everlasting monuments of our forefathers' devotion, consecrated to pious uses"'.

We may well feel sceptical about the qualities he attributes to particular rhythms; the whole question of the expressive effects of prose rhythm must be discussed later. All that matters at the moment is that it has been one focus of critical attention, the other having been the beauty of rhythms simply as patterns of sound and articulatory movement. With these as their focal points of interest it was inevitable that both Saintsbury and Croll should concentrate their attention on the more emotive or decorative or oratorical prose and even within that on the more elevated and moving passages. The connective tissue, the continuity, was largely neglected; and, more unfortunately, other kinds of prose were regarded, at least by Saintsbury, as rhythmically negligible or even deplorable.

The freeing of prose from the more obtrusive patterns of rhythm that draw attention to themselves and away from the sense, or that reinforce the sense with an emotive emphasis better suited to oratory than disinterested argument, is a more positive achievement than a writer with Saintsbury's preferences could admit. Sprat and the ideals of prose he encouraged in the Royal Society make no appeal to him and he has little use for what he calls the triumph of plainness in the latter half of the seventeenth century. It shows what a gulf there can be between views on the quality of prose that in 1932 an American psychologist, Gardner Murphy, wrote of John Locke 'He was gentle and delightful in his exposition, clear and easy to read', while just twenty years earlier Saintsbury had said that Locke '... for almost the first time makes English prose positively *mean* in every point of style, and in rhythm most of all' (p. 229).

It is worth while to look at a sentence in which Locke stated his purpose. In outline paraphrase it falls into three parts: (a) If I can demonstrate the limits of human understanding (b) I may persuade people (c) to give up trying to exceed them. In its full form the sentence runs

If by this inquiry into the nature of the understanding, I can discover the powers thereof, *how far* they reach, to what things they are in any degree proportionate, and where they fail us, I suppose it may be of use to prevail with the busy mind of man to be more cautious in meddling with things exceeding its comprehension, to stop when it is at the utmost of its tether, and to sit down in quiet ignorance of those things which, upon examination, are found to be beyond the reach of our capacities.

*(An Essay Concerning Human Understanding)*

The middle section, which I paraphrased 'I may persuade people', is a characteristically muted expression of deliberately (and ironically) moderate expectations –

I suppose it may be of use to prevail with the busy mind of man –

with very slight differences of stress, the rhythm units flowing into one another to give almost unpausing continuity. Once attuned to the frequency of light stresses and the long continued runs, we receive more effect from the few points of fairly heavy stress –

to stóp when it is at the útmost of its téther –

and from the occasional short and slightly more emphatic rhythm units –

*how far* they reach. . .and where they fail us. . .and to sit down. . .

The rhythmical qualities contribute to an evenness of tone consistent with low-pitched expectations, with the insertion of provisos ('things which, upon examination, are found. . .'), and with reasonable rather than forceful communication.

It would be imperceptive to suppose that rhythms like Locke's are accidental or arrive in the natural course of his expressing himself. The idea that we have been speaking prose all our lives is a delusion: a transcribed tape recording of ordinary speech shows at once what extensive tidying up must be done before prose emerges; conversely, if you read prose aloud, even simple prose, and try to make it sound like spontaneous speech you find you can't. The continuity of prose, the more complex sentences, the economy, the absence of false starts and blind alleys, and the longer uninterrupted blocks of utterance make the two things different. The exceptions – committeemen's smoothnesses, after-dinner speeches, stories by raconteurs, and very often lectures – these are prosings, prose masquerading as speech. (This is to adopt the standards of current speaking convention; it is possible that eighteenth century speaking was more formal among educated people, but the evidence is not easy to assess.)

Saintsbury gives no aid towards an understanding of the rhythmical organization of ordinary 'prosaic' prose. Below the 'highly rhythmed prose' that he most admired he recognized what he called 'sectional prose', illustrating it by setting out a passage from Burke in what amount to free verse lines:

> To complain of the age we live in,
> to murmur at the present possessors of power,
> to lament the past,
> to conceive extravagant hopes of the future –
> are the common dispositions of the greater part of mankind;
> indeed, the necessary effects of the ignorance and levity of the vulgar.

He comments 'Here, as the typographical disposition will have shown at once, there is rhythm, but rhythm attained almost solely by the parallelism of the members, and the difference of their length and terminations' (p. 275). Below sectional prose came 'the lower kinds of prose' (p. 346), some with their 'mean' rhythms, in which he showed no interest.

Although his account of the different 'levels' of prose is confused there can be no doubt that what he valued was a constant approach towards, and avoidance of, metrical writing. For reasons not clear to me he believed that prose like the passage from Burke was not susceptible of being analysed into 'feet'. In contrast, highly rhythmed prose 'is fully, and in every syllable, susceptible of quantification and consequent foot-scansion...Its great law is that every syllable shall, as in poetry, have recognised rhythmical value, and be capable of entering into rhythmical transactions with its neighbours, but that these transactions shall always stop short, or steer clear, of admitting the recurrent combinations proper to metre' (p. 344).

He failed to see that the creation of a prose still further removed from metre can be a positive achievement, certainly not to be reached by a disregard for rhythm. Shakespeare needed such a prose in order to secure an unmistakable contrast with the verse of the plays; the verse, everyone agrees, retains much of speech rhythm, but the prose – though it too must suggest spoken language – needs to present a perceptible contrast with the verse if it is to serve a special purpose. Look at Hotspur's soliloquy from the First Part of *Henry IV* as he reads the letter from a cautious gentleman who declines to join in the rebellion:

> Say you so, say you so? I say unto you again
> You are a shallow, cowardly hind, and you lie,
> What a lack-brain is this! By the Lord,
> Our plot is a good plot as ever was laid;
> Our friends true and constant: a good plot,
> Good friends, and full of expectation;
> An excellent plot, very good friends.
> What a frosty-spirited rogue is this!

At first glance it may be a little difficult to feel sure that this is not Shakespearian verse but Shakespeare's prose cut up into free verse lines. The rhythm units are short, the stresses strong and close together. But although not very clearly distinguished from one sort of verse the passage is probably more effective in its prose form. Printed in verse lines, the middle section loses something of its speed and rather desperate emphasis:

By the Lord, our plot is a good plot as ever was laid; our friends true and constant; a good plot, good friends, and full of expectation; an excellent plot, very good friends.

The rush and impetuosity, and the over-emphasis of a man who wants to reassure himself, are conveyed better through the continuity of the prose than they can be when line endings introduce even slight pauses.

In Hamlet's letter about the pirates, again, the units both of sense and of rhythm are short and rather sharply divided from each other, with an effect not entirely remote from verse:

Horatio, when thou shalt have overlooked this, give these fellows some means to the King: they have letters for him. Ere we were two days old at sea, a pirate of very warlike appointment gave us chase. Finding ourselves too slow of sail, we put on a compelled valour: in the grapple I boarded them: on the instant they got clear of our ship, so I alone became their prisoner...

There are even metrical intrusions:

Ere we were two days old at sea...
Finding ourselves too slow of sail...
so I alone became their prisoner...

In *Measure for Measure* the intensely emotional verse of the prison scene between Isabella and Claudio, when the horror of death shakes him, is followed immediately by the scene between Isabella and the disguised Duke in which prose is used for expounding the improbable plot to the audience, with a retrospect of the relations between Angelo and Mariana, a sketch of the plan for tricking him, and an attempt to justify it morally. For these purposes the dialogue brings a deliberate slowing in the current of the play's action. Most of the prose so studiously avoids any approach to metrical flow that it becomes stiff and more ponderous than natural speech even for a serious occasion:

*Duke.* Might you dispense with your leisure, I would by and by have some speech with you: the satisfaction I would require is likewise your own benefit.
*Isabella.* I have no superfluous leisure; my stay must be stolen out of other affairs; but I will attend you awhile.

But in its stiff way it is a plain prose for clear communication, avoiding decorative rhythm and securing far greater lucidity than much sixteenth century prose:

*Duke.* This forenamed maid hath yet in her the continuance of her first affection: his unjust unkindness, that in all reason should have quench'd her love, hath, like an impediment in the current, made it more violent and unruly. Go you to Angelo; answer his requiring with a plausible obedience; agree with his demands to the point. Only refer yourself to this advantage: first, that your stay with him may not be long; that the place may have all shadow and silence in it; and the time answer to convenience.

Even in such deliberately contrived prose some metrical residues still lurk:

The hand that hath made you fair hath made you good...
redeem your brother from the angry law...
She should this Angelo have married...
Can this be so? did Angelo so leave her?
and he, a marble to her tears, is wash'd with them...

By the time we reach *The Winter's Tale*, although the verse has been so largely freed from regular metre, the prose stands apart from it much more distinctively:

Sicilia cannot show himself over-kind to Bohemia. They were trained together in their childhoods; and there rooted between them such an affection, which cannot choose but branch now. Since their more mature dignities and royal necessities made separation of their society, their encounters, though not personal, have been royally attorneyed with interchange of gifts, letters, loving embassies; that they have seemed to be together, though absent; shook hands, as over a vast; and embraced, as it were, from the ends of opposed winds. The heavens continue their loves!

The prose now is toughly resistant to any tampering that could make it seem in delivery like verse:

So much, Camillo, have I considered, and with care; so far, that I have eyes which for my service look upon his removedness; from whom I learn that he is seldom from the house of a most homely shepherd; one that from very nothing, and beyond his neighbours' dreams, is grown to unspeakable estate.

I have in fact tampered with that passage, in which Polixenes speaks about Florizel's absences from court. The true version, the second of each pair of lines below, insists on a less iambic pattern of reading and also produces longer sense units and less sharply marked units of speech rhythm:

So much, Camillo, have I considered, and with care; so far
I have considered so much, Camillo, and with some care; so far

that I have eyes which for my service look upon his removedness;
that I have eyes under my service which look upon his removedness;

from whom I learn that he is seldom from the house
from whom I have this intelligence, that he is seldom from the house

of a most homely shepherd; one that from very nothing,
of a most homely shepherd; a man, they say, that from very nothing,

and beyond his neighbours' dreams,
and beyond the imagination of his neighbours,

is grown to unspeakable estate.
is grown into an unspeakable estate.

Naturally the unemphatic continuity gained by the long runs of lightly stressed syllables without much pausing is specially appropriate to the roles of the king and the courtier in consultation. But the same avoidance of anything like verse rhythms is to be found in the different prose of the dialogue between Volumnia and Virgilia in *Coriolanus*: for instance:

I pray you, daughter, sing; or express yourself in a more comfortable sort: if my son were my husband, I should freelier rejoice in that absence wherein he won honour than in the embracements of his bed where he would show most love.

In speeches like this Shakespeare was producing – gradually produced – a prose that stands clearly apart from his verse. Although it retains the quality of speech, in one register or another, it is a strictly controlled, deliberately created form of language, avoiding any hint of submerged metre in its rhythms.

The rhythmical 'meanness' that Saintsbury found in such prose as Locke's was one aspect of a chosen style of writing adapted to particular outlooks and purposes. To view it as a lapse, a failure to achieve the rich curves and gestures of 'ornate' prose, was a touch of Saintsbury's parochialism of period. And a recognition of its positive merits is far from implying that any casual outflow of prose utterance can be rhythmically justified. As in appreciating the achievements of free verse, so here in prose, although we have discarded Saintsbury's particular partialities and aversions, we must be prepared to say what kind of rhythm is *not* satisfactory, and why.

The awkwardness we feel in a rhythm is at times the first indication that something has gone wrong with the structure of the sentence. Cyril Connolly, discussing a British civil servant who worked for Russian espionage, wrote:

This fits in with Donald's character. He is said to have disappeared once from a party for a few days in Switzerland and been found living quietly in the next village. (*Sunday Times*, 28 September 1952)

The rhythm carries you with a kind of gallop through 'He is said to have disappeared once from a party', followed by another phrase, 'for a few days in Switzerland'. But the sense, as far as it can be guessed at, is that the *party* was in Switzerland (since if he had left a party in England 'for a few days in Switzerland' he would not be said to have 'disappeared'). It seems to be a case where an ambiguous sentence, presumably written in the haste of journalism, becomes more misleading from the fact that its rhythms firmly unite words that shouldn't go together and help to separate those that should. A similar trouble occurs in the title of a paper, 'Anniversary reactions in parents precipitated by children' (*Psychiatry*, 1953, 16: 73–80). Because 'Anniversary reactions' makes a unit of both sense and rhythm, within a long title, the inclination is to pause there momentarily, and then meet the phrase 'of parents precipitated by children', with its bizarre suggestions.

Rather than spending time on minor pieces of carelessness it may be more rewarding to look at the usually good utilitarian prose – as Saintsbury would have called it – of a book that came out six years before his *History of English Prose Rhythm*. Sherrington's classic work, *The Integrative Action of the Nervous System*, is generally pleasant to read as well as clear; but here and there a slight awkwardness seems to be due to the rhythm. A passage dealing with the adaptive value of reflexes goes well until the last sentence:

Perfected during the course of ages, they have during that course attained a stability, a certainty, and an ease of performance beside which the stability and facility of the most ingrained habit acquired during an individual life is presumably small. But theirs is of itself a machine-like fatality. Their character in this stands revealed when the neural arcs which execute them are separated, e.g. by transection of the spinal cord, from the higher centres of the nervous system. They can be checked, it is true, as we have seen, by collision with other reflexes as ancestral and as fatally operative as themselves. (p. 388)

There is an uncomfortable jerkiness about 'They can be checked, it is true, as we have seen'; any two of these units could have been used together satisfactorily, but three in succession, similar in rhythm, firmly separated by punctuation and each ending on a stress, too sharply hold up the flow of the sentence. A superficially similar sentence, but with more varied rhythms in the sub-units, flows without jerkiness:

It was, after all, true in a sense, that Madeline did want to be friends...
(L. H. Myers, *The Orissers*, p. 160)

And further on in Sherrington's sentence one hesitates a moment before discovering how to accentuate 'other reflexes as ancestral...' It would be easy enough to rewrite the sentence in a way that produces mere smoothness:

It is true, as we have seen, that they can be checked by collision with other reflexes no less ancestral and fatally operative than themselves.

This would give the rhythmical nullity of an official memorandum. Sherrington wanted a crisper start to the sentence, a sharp proviso modifying the preceding generalization; but that created a rhythmical problem he failed to solve. In the spoken form of the lectures on which the book is based he may have salvaged the sentence by his timing and intonation of the sub-units, but in printed form it has a jerkiness that serves no purpose.

His next page illustrates the opposite trouble – a sentence offering a long stream of syllables with insufficient rhythmical structure to provide any help in marking the sense units:

The transition from reflex action to volition is not abrupt and sharp. Familiar instances of individual acquisition of motor co-ordination are furnished by the cases in which short, simple movements, whether reflex or not, are by practice under volition combined into new sequences and become in time habitual in the sense that though able to be directed they no longer require concentration of attention upon them for their execution.

It is by contrast with a sentence like that that one can appreciate the rhythmical shaping of Locke's apparently casual run of syllables:

I suppose it may be of use to prevail with the busy mind of man to be more cautious in meddling with things exceeding its comprehension. . .

Again it may be that in the spoken lectures Sherrington's long sentence would have been given more shape by pauses and pitch changes than it seems to have in print. But in fact very small changes would give even the printed sentence a clearer rhythmical structure:

Familiar instances of the individual acquisition of motor co-ordination are furnished by the cases in which short, simple movements, whether reflex or not, are combined into new sequences by practice under volition and become in time habitual in the sense that, though they can be directed, concentration of attention upon them is no longer needed for their execution.

In all prose, utilitarian included, the words are being grouped into patterns according to two systems, simultaneously operative: patterns of sense and syntax, and patterns of sound and movement. If these two systems of patterning come into conflict some uneasiness occurs, and if the conflict is serious the effect is of disjointedness and dislocation.

Not that smoothness has to be the aim. Deliberate interruptions, breaks in the flowing sentence structure and its rhythmical continuity, may serve the writer's special ends. For instance in F. R. Leavis's prose there is often a considered 'jaggedness', in which subordinate clauses and parentheses break abruptly into the main line of thought with the effect of hinting at the complexity and the over-abundant context out of which any simple statement is disentangled, and of shunning with qualifications and unexpected enlargements the lenitive roundedness of administrators' prose (and thinking). However, that aspect of rhythm in emphasizing characteristics of a writer's thought merges with the more general question, still to be discussed, of the expressive significance of rhythm in prose.

# 10

# Expressive effects of prose rhythm

Rhythm is so intimately fused with sense in any meaningful utterance that it must always be difficult, often impossible, to be sure how much it contributes to the total expressive effect. With prose an initial problem arises in even identifying the rhythm whose effects we want to examine. Are we to work in 'feet', with Saintsbury; or with Croll to note the numerical position of stressed syllables from the end of a sentence or clause; or simply to show by spacing and accent marks (or by symbols such as Stannard Allen used for language teaching) where the main runs and pauses and emphases occur? All such methods must remain sketchy and clumsy compared with any scheme for registering with full comprehensiveness the way a passage is spoken, with degrees of stress, patterns of pitch change, duration of syllables, varying length of pause between words, and the tempo of the speech with its accelerations and decelerations. Such efforts as have been made at complete comprehensiveness may serve specialized purposes for language analysts and phoneticians, but for more general use they are not attractive, since they require the learning of a new and complicated system of signs, a considerably more difficult notation than music.

For most purposes of literary discussion it is enough to note the main features of grouping and stress, supplementing these when necessary with a verbal description of tempo and its variations, quality of 'attack' and so forth. For my purpose it is generally enough to divide the chief rhythmical units by spacing and to show the main stresses by accent marks – admittedly conveying only a broad outline of the rhythm and neglecting the many points where a slight pause or a slight difference of stress may create a subordinate division within a long run of syllables. Individual readers mark or perceive these minor features to a different degree. There will usually be something arbitrary, for instance, in judging how many distinguishable rhythmical units occur in a given passage.

A further difficulty in examining the expressive effects of rhythm, again in prose especially (though it can be important in verse too), is to decide on the length of the passage which can be perceived as a rhythmical whole. The small nuclear units, integral to the spoken language, are unquestionably facts of immediate perception. A short sentence or clause, with sense and punctuation to distinguish it from its flowing context, will usually be perceived as having rhythmical unity. What of a paragraph or a long, sustained sentence? In a paragraph of quiet, rational argument, without sharp breaks in the flow or strongly marked differences of stress, there may either be no overall rhythmical organization or what there is may be so slightly defined that it grows apparent only after several readings. When, however, the syntactical or the rhythmical sections are clearly related to one another, for instance by repetition (or approximate repetition) of the same structure, by a cumulative array of similar or developing structures, or by repetitions succeeded by the sudden check of a contrast, then the paragraph as a whole will have an immediately perceptible rhythmic unity:

But when vague rumours got abroad, that in this Protestant association a secret power was mustering against the government for undefined and mighty purposes; when the air was filled with whispers of a confederacy among the Popish powers to degrade and enslave England, establish an Inquisition in London, and turn the pens of Smithfield Market into stakes and cauldrons; when terrors and alarms which no man understood were perpetually broached, both in and out of Parliament, by one enthusiast who did not understand himself, and bygone bugbears which had lain quietly in their graves for centuries, were raised again to haunt the ignorant and credulous; when all this was done, as it were, in the dark, and secret invitations to join the Great Protestant Association in defence of religion, life and liberty, were dropped in the public ways, thrust under the house-doors, tossed in at windows, and pressed into the hands of those who trod the streets by night; when they glared from every wall, and shone on every post and pillar, so that stocks and stones appeared infected with the common fear, urging all men to join together blindfold in resistance of they knew not what, they knew not why; – then the mania spread indeed, and the body, still increasing every day, grew forty thousand strong.

(*Barnaby Rudge*, Chapter XXXVII)

Even with a paragraph like this there is some doubt whether we really grasp the rhythmical movement as a fact of direct, unreflective experience. I think we do; if so, it is something different from an intellectual understanding of the structure of the passage such as inspection and analysis can yield. It may quite often be that when re-reading and reflection have shown us the way in which a paragraph has been constructed we then pass to a more direct experience of its pattern of movement; and of course individual differences in the perceiver (including his experience and practice) will count heavily.

Beyond the paragraph it seems most unlikely that we get any direct perception of the unity and patterning of a long piece of writing – the structure of a novel, for instance, or even the pattern of one of Donne's sermons. Instead there is a reflective grasp of structure: observation and retrospective survey show that a large section of a work, possibly the whole work, has a unity of patterned divisions, recurrent points of tension or heightened speed, a succession of increasingly emotional climaxes, perhaps a post-climactic repose, and all this will be analogous to a rhythmical pattern. C. K. Munro (1933), for instance, analysing *The Wild Duck*, showed diagrammatically, with curves, the pattern of fluctuating but developing suspense that Ibsen created. Although the pattern is analogous to a rhythm, and each phase is experienced by the playgoer in heightenings and relaxations of tension as the play proceeds, the total pattern is not experienced as an immediate perceptual whole – it has to be surveyed and thought about. We could make a diagram of the stages of human life, with its periods of accelerated growth, its fluctuations of physical activity and rest, its gradual decline in vigour; these stages are directly experienced, and in retrospect they can be viewed as a pattern, but the pattern is not unreflectively perceived as a fact of experience in the way that we do, for instance, unreflectively perceive the tick-tock of a grandfather clock or the unity of a line of verse.

A writer's plan and general approach will in part be expressed in the broad structure and main divisions of his novel, his treatise, his sermon... A competent writer's paragraphs will be at least compatible with the construction of his larger divisions, his chapters, for instance. In a writer of distinction there is likely also to be compatibility, and perhaps mutual reinforcement, between on the one hand characteristic qualities of his approach to the subject, his broad patterning of his material, and on the other the directly perceivable rhythm of his prose. It is difficult not to believe that passages we feel to be specially characteristic of a writer owe something of this to their quality of rhythm. Some of the torrentially abundant and cumulative sentences of Dickens, for instance, are part and parcel of his creative prodigality and expansiveness. And a sentence such as the one just quoted from *Barnaby Rudge* could scarcely have been used to convey the subtleties and the gradual unfoldings of situation and attitude that make a late novel by Henry James.

There are, when one comes to look for them, fewer of the long, intricately unwinding sentences in Henry James than the parodists imply. More usual are sentences of fairly simple rhythm that gain their complexity of meaning from what they refer to in the context of the novel, sentences that advance with only slight divagations to the firmly rhythmical close of a simple pattern. The kind of pattern can be seen in two sentences of Densher's reflections in *The Wings of the Dove* when he is walking with Kate and feels an irrational uneasiness, as if his deceitful relation with the dying Milly had become public knowledge:

Only Kate, at all events knew – what Kate did know, and she was also the last person interested to tell it; in spite of which it was as if his *act*, so deeply associated with her and never to be recalled nor recovered, was abroad on the winds of the world. His honesty, as he viewed it, with Kate, was the very element of that menace: to the degree that he saw at moments, as to their final impulse or their final remedy, the need to bury in the dark blindness of each other's arms the knowledge of each other that they couldn't undo.

(Chapter XXXVIII)

The hesitations and breaks – 'at all events knew – what Kate did know' – and the careful qualifications – 'His honesty, as he viewed it, with Kate' – and the variation between short and long clauses, all these devices of suspense and preparation lead to a simple concluding rhythm (in fact in the first sentence a lapse into metre): 'was abroad on the winds of the world'; 'the knowledge of each other that they couldn't undo'.

And even the occasional long sentences, those that do lend themselves to the usual parody, wind their way through delaying extensions and refinements to the same kind of rather simple rhythmic close; as for example in Densher's impression of the dying girl when she receives him in Venice:

Her welcome, her frankness, sweetness, sadness, brightness, her disconcerting poetry, as he made shift at moments to call it, helped as it was by the beauty of her whole setting and by the perception, at the same time, on the observer's part, that this element gained from her, in a manner, for effect and harmony, as much as it gave – her whole attitude had, to his imagination, meanings that hung about it, waiting upon her, hovering, dropping, and quavering forth again, like vague, faint snatches, mere ghosts of sound, of old-fashioned melancholy music.

(Chapter XXVI)

These concluding rhythms –

the knowledge of each other that they couldn't undo
of old-fashioned melancholy music

– are quite different from the liturgical patterns identified by Croll, but like them they have a clear shape and a continuous flow and so reinforce the clinching effect towards which James works by way of his long preparatory delays.

A different form, and a different use, of a sustained, accumulating sentence structure is seen in some of Jane Austen's sentences, where the succession of items is allowed to come to an apparent close, but is then followed by a short addition which has the effect of an ironic or comic addendum. Some of the sentences that are always remembered are of this kind. When Henry Tilney has been instructing Catherine in the picturesque we get one of these effects:

Delighted with her progress, and fearful of wearying her with too much wisdom at once, Henry suffered the subject to decline, and by an easy transition from a piece of rocky fragment and the withered oak which he had placed near its summit, to oaks in general, to forests, the inclosure of them, waste lands, crown lands and government, he shortly found himself arrived at politics;

then, after the rhythmical close and the semicolon, the addendum:

and from politics, it was an easy step to silence.

The same movement of sentences occurs during Emma's reflections on the party at the Coles, when she feels a little uneasy on two points. One is whether she behaved unfairly in discussing Jane Fairfax's supposed feelings with Frank Churchill. On the second point she is more definite:

The other circumstance of regret related also to Jane Fairfax; and there she had no doubt. She did unfeignedly and unequivocally regret the inferiority of her own playing and singing. She did most heartily grieve over the idleness of her childhood –

stopped at that point we have three sentences of somewhat similar pattern reinforcing each other and coming to what seems like an emphatic and conclusive statement of regret. But then, after the dash, comes the addendum with its anticlimax:

and sat down and practised vigorously an hour and a half.

Not only does the sense of 'vigorously' make its ironic comment on Emma's personality (like the lists of books she intended to read) but the light run of syllables 'vigorously an hour and a half' contributes its own part to the effect of mockery. Much would have been lost if the sentence had run

She did most heartily grieve over the idleness of her childhood – and sat down and practised hard for an hour.

I think the total movement of short passages like these from Jane Austen is, or becomes on re-reading, a perceivable rhythm.

The added phrase, following what could have been a completed unit of sense and rhythm, was a conspicuous feature of Gibbon's armoury, as Croll points out. Croll speaks (p. 341) of Gibbon's use of 'words – added as if by an afterthought – that follow the cadenced phrase', for example,

Dadastana was marked as the fatal term of his journey (planus) and his life.

In this example it is the sense of the words that leads us to make an addendum of 'and his life'. If the sense is altered a much more continuous flow becomes possible:

Dadastana was marked as the joyful term of his journey and his quest.

The same 'planus' remains, but the pitch pattern and the slight pause after 'journey' that made it seem like a conclusion are no longer there; the sense determines the rhythm, but once the rhythm has been adopted it can strengthen the emotion or attitude that the sense evokes. When a final phrase is handled as an addendum or afterthought its own rhythmical characteristics help to determine or strengthen its expressive value; and they may vary widely, as the examples from Jane Austen and Gibbon testify.

In prose as in verse the likelihood is that expressive rhythm is an aspect of energy output. Amplitude, suddenness, variations in the rate of discharge, smooth continuity or intermittency, such features of energy expenditure as these can show themselves in rhythm, and they are likely to reflect states of mind and body such as excitement, calm, uncertainty and hesitation, confident assurance, determination, vigour, lassitude and so on.

The sustaining of a movement, the building up and the point of pause, will affect the force given to the sense of the words that occur at various stages of the process. When Saintsbury says of the phrase from Burton – 'those fair buildings and everlasting monuments of our forefathers' devotion, consecrated to pious uses' – that 'The rhythm more than suits, it positively heightens, the sense', we may well ask how it can possibly do anything of the sort. The 'sense' of the descriptive phrase is there in the words and cannot be heightened. Presumably Saintsbury meant that the emotion evoked by the sense is heightened – the kind of evaluation implied by the key words of 'fair', 'everlasting', 'devotion', 'consecrated'. The force of these words is affected by their place in the rhythmical whole. The sense would have been the same in the form, 'those fair buildings, consecrated to pious uses, and everlasting monuments of our forefathers' devotion'; but the emotional force would have been much less. The original form builds up with a continuous swinging movement; there are rhythmical sub-units, with very slight pauses after 'buildings' and 'monuments', but they merge into a continuity which creates a large rhythmical span, with a hint of the incantatory, before the word 'devotion' comes as a climax and a resting place; and the pause there gives additional force to the word that follows, 'consecrated'.

There is no reason to think that this particular sustained movement enhances only the 'solemn' emotion that Burton was suggesting: its long swing and culminating emphasis could accord with and strengthen other attitudes, pleading, for instance, or nostalgic longing, and probably many others. It seems to be the form of the emotional process as it develops, rather than its particular quality, that rhythms of this kind convey.

The idea that rhythms have expressive value will easily be discredited if we take it to mean that a particular rhythm is peculiarly appropriate to one emotion rather than another. That this is not so is even more obvious in speech and prose than in verse. 'I adore her', 'I abhor her', 'It's appalling', 'It's enthralling', all these phrases with their diverse emotional value share the same rhythmical form; and we cannot even claim that this form is specially appropriate to emphatic utterance, since it will serve just as well for neutral phrases such as 'In the meanwhile', 'Can I help you?', 'Will you show me?'. Naturally, the greater part of the texture of speech and prose has to be emotionally neutral or low-toned – otherwise we should be in a state of perpetual excitement in all communication. It is only when a phrase is isolated or emphasized by one means or another, and its emotional value defined by intonation, timing, degree of differentiation in stress, and other qualities of speech, that its rhythm too may contribute appreciably to the total effect. So we might say 'His hands were full and he couldn't open the door without dropping something', where 'open the door', which could be a sharply defined rhythmical unit, is embedded as an emotionally neutral part of the continuum. Much the same is true of bodily movement; most of it, most of the time, is non-expressive, and only occasionally does part of it stand out as a gesture or a significant posture.

Comparing the rhythms of prose with those of bodily movement points to a distinction, touched on in Chapter 4, that needs to be made and is often neglected. A movement, or a sequence of movements, or the whole style of a person's movement may be graceful or clumsy and in some measure pleasing or disagreeable to watch, regardless of any expressive value it may have. This can be called the 'aesthetic' aspect of the movement, for want of a word less open to misunderstanding. It is distinguishable from the expressive value which converts a movement into a gesture, and which makes a posture or a style of moving significant of an attitude or emotion or a mode of deploying energy. In the parallel case of prose it is the general aesthetic quality that Saintsbury implies when he praises 'ornate' and 'highly rhythmed' writing and deplores mean rhythms and the triumph of the plain style. And it is in the appraisal of this aspect of prose that personal preferences and fluctuating fashions count for most. So Morley (1877, p. 397) could exclaim '...turn to a page of Macaulay and wince under its stamping emphasis,...its unlovely staccato'.

Although the aesthetic and the expressive aspects of prose rhythm need to be distinguished they are often, as one would expect, closely allied. Synge's writing illustrates the point. There is an appeal, a charm rather quickly exhausted, in the lilting rhythms of the synthetic Anglo-Irish which he derived by way of Lady Gregory from

Douglas Hyde's literal translations of Irish idiom. Its obvious
fabrication and its facile attractiveness come out clearly in his translations from Petrarch and Villon; for example:

The hair that was of shining gold, and brightness of the smile that was the like
of an angel's surely, and was making a paradise of the earth, are turned to a little
dust that knows nothing at all.

*(Poems and Translations)*

But although the rhythm of such a passage has its general charm it
also has some expressive value that makes it appropriate to certain
ranges of subject matter and not others. Synge when he wanted could
write straightforward English; he kept his special Anglo-Irish for
the more romantic and nostalgic themes and for the sake of giving
piquancy to the everyday remarks of ordinary characters in his plays.
But within that broad range of appropriate subject matter and purpose, focal points of emotion occurred for which he sought specially
fitting rhythmical expression.

His shaping of a rhythm to enhance the emotional quality of a
particular statement can be watched in the stages leading to the final
form of the speech that ends *Riders to the Sea*. It took its origin in a
letter, quoted by Greene and Stephens (1959), which he received
from one of his Irish friends whose brother Shawneen had lost his
wife:

And she was visiting the last Sunday in December, and now isn't it a sad story to
tell? But at the same time we have to be satisfied because a person cannot live
always. But Shawneen is good, but he is very lonely. But if he is, he has to be
satisfied. (p. 105)

From this – in which natural speech is no doubt distorted in some
degree by unskilled letter writing – Synge took, first, the recognition
that no one can live for ever; and, second, the choice of the word
'satisfied' to convey the idea of acceptance and resignation. In the
draft of a play, apparently unpublished, one of Synge's characters,
according to Greene and Stephens,

distinctly echoes Martin McDonough's words about his brother's tragedy – 'I'm
destroyed crying; but what good is in it? We must be satisfied and what man at
all can be living for ever?' (p. 116)

With this version he has achieved much of the familiar lilting effect.
Rhythmically he has made a more compact unit in 'must be satisfied'
instead of 'has to be satisfied', and one which (by avoiding the run of

quick syllables, 'has to be') accords better with the sombre mood; 'person' has become 'man' (a shift towards the Biblical) with the addition of 'at all' helping to produce the swing of this special language; and 'be living for ever' creates a similar swing out of the bare 'live always' of the letter. In the final revision, the moving last words of *Riders to the Sea*, he considerably moderates the theatre Irish and gets much greater finality into the rhythm by abandoning the question form and ending on the shorter of the two statements:

Bartley will have a fine coffin out of the white boards, and a deep grave surely. What more can we want than that? No man at all can be living for ever, and we must be satisfied.

The last sentence has hints of an approach to metre (with something of the movement of 'Take her up tenderly, Lift her with care'), but the speech pauses sufficiently break up the repetitive dactyls, and they contribute only obscurely if at all to the satisfying unity of the sentence. Many processes went to the creation of this special theatre prose out of the suggestion in Martin McDonough's letter, but one of them, an important one, was the gradual reshaping of the rhythm.

In all our judgements about the expressive quality of a rhythm we are guessing and fumbling; there is no certainty that the rhythm is doing more to us than we, with our subjective interpretation, are doing to it. And if someone else fails to experience it as we do, or interprets it differently, that may or may not be because he is insufficiently sensitive or practised. Experimental work on the expressive quality of language rhythms seems not to have been done, although good instrumental resources are now available; and it should be possible, for instance, to identify characteristic rhythmical patterns, if there are any, arising in known emotional states. Lacking evidence of this kind, however, we can at least examine fairly spontaneous prose, in letters and diaries, written in identifiable moods. Negative evidence would not be conclusive; lack of rhythmical expressiveness might point only to the stiffness or ineptness of the writer's English. But writers with a good command of English may be expected – if rhythm is expressive – to produce rhythms that accord with their mood.

Two passages from Dorothy Osborne's *Letters* (ed. Moore Smith, 1928), written in sharply contrasting moods, seem to be rhythmically expressive and very different. The differences are not easy to specify, but perhaps some approach is worth attempting. I indicate (with accent marks for stressed syllables, a superior point for minor pauses, and a virgule for major pauses) the rhythm I adopt for the passages; variations between one reader and another (and two readings by the same person) will not be great enough to invalidate the broad comparisons I want to make. The first passage comes from a letter written in great depression (which seems to have been genuine notwithstanding its histrionic elements) when her love affair with Temple had met with such formidable obstructions that she decided to end their secret engagement, and this had made him write reproaching her. Part of her unhappy reply runs

I shall práy that yóu · may Obtáin a quíett, · Í never hópe for · but ín my gráve, / and I shall néver · Chánge my condítion · but wíth my life. / Yet lét not thís · gíve you a hópe, / nóthing can éver perswáde mee · to énter the wórlde agáine, / I sháll in a shórt tíme · have disingáged my sélf · of áll my lítle affáires in it / and séttled my sélf · in a condítion to aprehénd nóthing · but tóo lóng a life, / thérfore I wísh · yóu would forgétt mee, / and to indúce you to it · lét mee téll you fréely · that I desérve you shóuld. / if I remémber ány bódy · tis agáinst my wíll, / I am posséssed · with that stránge insencibíllity · that my néerest relátions · have nóe týe ypon mee, / and I fínde my self · nóe móre concérned · in thóse that I have hertofóre · had gréat téndernesse of afféction for / then in my kíndred that dýed · lóng before Í was bórne.

(Letter 50, 31 December 1653)

This letter produced such a crisis that Dorothy gave way and renewed her commitment to him. Three weeks later she was writing in a very different vein. She had been telling him about a rival admirer whom she was keeping at a distance:

fýe, / what a déal of páper · have I spént ypon this ídle fféllow, / if I had thóught his stórry · would have próved soe lóng / you should have míssed on't / and the Lósse would nót have bin gréat. / I have nót · thánked you yét · for my twéeses and éssences, / they are bóth · véry góod, / I képt · óne of the litle glásses · my sélf; / remémber my ríng / and in retóurne / if Í goe to Lóndon · whilest yóu are in Íreland / i'le háve my Pícture táken in litle · and sénd it you. / the sóoner you dispátch awáy · will bee the bétter I thínk, / since I have nóe hópes · of séeing you befóre you góe; / thére lyes áll your buísnesse, / your fáther & fórtune · must dóe the rést, / I cannot bée / more yours then I am. . .

(Letter 55, 21 January 1653/4)

Subjectively the impression is of a plodding weariness in the first passage and a brisk eagerness in the second. Looked at more closely, the plodding effect of the first is largely due to the frequency with which the units of rhythm end with the pattern 'da-de-da': práy that yóu, Obtáin a quíett, but ín my gráve, but wíth my lífe, Yet lét not thís, the worlde agáine, disingáged my sélf, too lóng a lífe, desérve you shóuld, agáinst my wíll, noe móre concérned. (I omit the last four units of the passage in order to have, for comparison, the same length as the second passage.) Against these eleven, the buoyant passage uses this rhythm only five or six times: have próved soe lóng, thánked you yét, véry góod (where the first stress is too light to give the plodding effect), befóre you góe, must dóe the rést, I cannot bée.

The greater liveliness of the second passage derives also from what seems to be greater variety in the units of rhythm that make it up. The length of the units is more varied: in the first passage there are no units of one, two or three syllables, 22 of four, five or six syllables, and 8 of seven or more syllables; in the second passage there are only 14 units in the middle range of four, five or six syllables, with 7 units of one, two or three syllables, and 9 of seven syllables or more. The sense of rhythmical variety in the second passage is contributed to further by the contrasting length of adjacent rhythmical units. This can be tested by noting the difference in the number of syllables between the first unit and the second, the second and the third, and so on, and totalling these differences: for the depressed passage the total is 53, for the second passage 74. There would be little point in attempting any statistical rigour or refinement in these comparisons, given the small amount of material and the element of subjectivity in dividing the passages into rhythmical units. But the analysis points in the direction of possible objective studies, and as far as it goes confirms the subjective impressions.

It would be no use applying these same measures, or any one system of calculation, to other pieces of prose. The rhythmical resources of language are too numerous and varied, and too complex in their possible interactions, to be handled in a simple framework of pre-arranged categories. Any expressive effect of rhythm must in the first place be experienced subjectively. Only if we then go on to say what features of the prose give rise to the perceived effect does it become useful to check in some objective way whether those features are really there in one passage and not there in another that we experience differently.

With this proviso it is worth while examining two emotionally contrasting passages from another fluent and spontaneous writer, B. R. Haydon, who serves well in this context because of his known manic-depressive personality and extreme fluctuations of mood. The *Diary* (ed. W. B. Pope, 1963) expresses in the main Haydon's conviction of his power as a painter, his determination to work, his vigorous protest at people and circumstances that thwart him – but it also records spells of depression and inertia, 'dreadful fits of sluggish disgust' (21 June 1829). Entries for May 1829 record the latter part of such a spell, with a long entry on 10 May:

Réad Práyers at hóme – / felt bítter remórse of cónscience · at my láte negléct. / It is extraórdinary · my infatuátion [fatuity, stupidity]. / I gó ón, · dáy after dáy, · like Jóhnson in hypochóndria, / lóoking for hóurs · like an ídiot · at my Pícture, · without the pówer to dó · óne síngle thíng. / With mý fámily · it is dréadful. / I am so óften · túrned off my bálance · by pecúniary dífficulty, / that it is a perpétual strúggle · to gét on the róad again, / and yet the ónly chánce I háve · of gétting out of dífficulty · is by hárd wórk, / & nów my héalth is só much recóvered · I óught not thús to díssipate · the fíne matúrity of my lífe. / 10 dáys are góne in Máy; / áll Ápril and áll Jánuary · I did nóthing. / Óh, · it is disgráceful! / Ó Gód, · assíst me to vánquish · this bítter delínquency · of infatuátion. / If I had réad – / if I had advánced my knówledge, / it would be wéll, / but I have dóne nóthing · but sít & múse · and buíld cástles, / till I awóke and músed agáin. / I can hardly réad · without sléeping.

He had probably begun to emerge from the depression when he wrote this, and a week later he was euphoric but made only a short entry in the diary.

But about ten months later, when he was at work on 'Xenophon and the Ten Thousand' and in a phase of elation in spite of material difficulties, there is an entry long enough to compare with that of 10 May. It occurs on 20 March 1830:

I shall nów · dáte my Xénophon, / for todáy, · Gód be práised, · I begán, / having got a bréathing day. / I dáshed in the efféct. / My mínd · téemed with expréssions: / the enthúsiasm of Xénophon · chéering on his mén, / with his hélmet · tówering against a séa ský! – / a beaútiful wóman · léaning on her húsband's bréast exhaústed, / in his árms, / héaring the shóut of · 'the Séa! · the Séa!' / lánguidly smíling · and ópening her lóvely eýes! / (góod Gód! / Whát I could dó · if I were encóuraged!) – / a wóunded & síck sóldier · ráising his pále héad, / & wáving his thín árm & hánd, / in ánswer to the chéer of his Commánder, – / hórses snórting & gálloping – / sóldiers chéering & huzzáing! – / áll strúggling to sée · the wélcome síght. / I'll réad áll the retréats – / Napóleon's, · Chárles XII's, · Móore's, · Ántony's, · &c. &c. / Gód spáre · my lífe & eýes. / I féar the intrígues of Seguíer · have for éver destróyed · áll próspects with my Kíng! / I'd inspíre him if I was néar him. / They áll knów thís, / & fróm hím they will kéep me. / In my Protéctor I trúst. / Ámén.

In these two passages the expressive value of the movement of the words, as an enhancement of the feelings evoked by their sense, seems unmistakable. The first, sober and rather steady in its progress, contrasts with the eager impulsiveness of the second with its leaps from one exclamatory emphasis to another. There is no great difference in the total number of rhythmical units in the two passages (44 in the first, 48 in the second); but in the major units – those rather sharply disjunct from the preceding and following units, marked in my notation by a virgule – the difference is substantial, 20 in the first passage, 28 in the second. The first passage, it is true, contains some exclamatory sentences – they came readily to Haydon –

It is extraordinary my infatuation.
Oh, it is disgraceful.
O God. . .
If I had read –

The vigour of these short rhythmical units suggests that, although in substance they are self-reproachful, Haydon was already beginning to climb out of the trough of his depression, confirming what is implied in the fact that he has managed to resume family prayers. But the second passage, besides being more exclamatory, has many more short rhythmical units: units of one, two or three syllables amount to 3 in the first passage and 14 in the second. And 41 per cent of the syllables in the second passage carry a strong stress, compared with just under 31 per cent in the first.

Apart from any count of this sort, the passages differ in the interaction of rhythmical with syntactical organization. In the second the successions of listed items ('horses snorting and galloping, soldiers cheering and huzzaing'; 'all the retreats – Napoleon's, Charles XII's …') help to create short, crisp, staccato units. Contrastingly, in the first passage, two long sentences and part of a third provide the keynote, most of their constituent rhythm units flowing rather easily and continuously into one another:

I go on, day after day, like Johnson in hypochondria, looking for hours like an idiot at my Picture, without the power to do one single thing.

I am so often turned off my balance by pecuniary difficulty, that it is a perpetual struggle to get on the road again, and yet the only chance I have of getting out of difficulty is by hard work, & now my health is so much recovered I ought not thus to dissipate the fine maturity of my life.

. . .but I have done nothing but sit & muse and build castles, till I awoke and mused again.

It is this subdued, continuous movement that contrasts with the thrust and sharp pulsation, ballistic and almost percussive, of the second passage. It is impossible not to feel that these movement patterns help to express the contrasting moods, however much the sense of the words is necessary to specify the moods more narrowly.

As material for exploring the expressive value of rhythm in prose, letters and diaries have special value on account of their relative spontaneity and nearness to the speech of identifiable emotional states. Few letter writers, however, will be so gifted in their control of English as Dorothy Osborne was. Lapses of skill in the letter writer or diarist can easily disturb potentially effective rhythms, just as the flow of natural speech itself can be broken while we hesitate or grope for words or correct ourselves. Moreover the exclamatory speech of many emotional states tends to be repetitive and lose some of its force through sameness. It follows that the kind of prose that aims at suggesting speech – especially the dialogue of plays and novels – is a highly artificial creation, and at its best is more flexible and concentrated in rhythm than natural speech itself.

One of the unquestionable achievements of the best Restoration comedy was a prose which outdid speech without becoming something different – greatly compressed and very fluent compared with everyday speaking, highly flexible and rhythmically varied, but still exploiting some of the short rhythm units, the pauses or breaks, and the abrupt junctures of natural speech in emotion. It can be found readily in *The Way of the World*; here is Lady Wishfort raging at the maid:

What, then I have been your Property, have I? I have been convenient to you, it seems, – while you were catering for *Mirabell*; I have been Broaker for you? What, have you made a passive Bawd of me? – This exceeds all Precedent; I am brought to fine Uses, to become a Botcher of second-hand Marriages between *Abigails* and *Andrews*! I'll couple you. Yes, I'll baste you together, you and your *Philander*. I'll *Duke's-Place* you, as I'm a Person. Your Turtle is in Custody already: you shall Coo in the same Cage, if there be Constable or Warrant in the Parish. (v, i.)

Much of the effectiveness of the passage comes from its rhythmical variety, the impetuous rush of the longer sentences, the sudden

blows of the short ones (I'll couple you'), the monosyllabic exclamations, the repetition of the same syntactical form with sharply
different rhythmical patterns ('I'll couple you. Yes, I'll baste you together, you and your *Philander*. I'll *Duke's-Place* you, as I'm a
Person.'). These are not the accidents of natural exclamation but
notably a created prose.

Its tense and flexible liveliness shows up the rhythmic repetitiveness and relative flaccidity, for all its exclamatory form, of the speech
of Oscar Wilde's Lady Chilton as she castigates her ideal husband:

Don't come near me. Don't touch me. I feel as if you had soiled me for ever.
Oh! what a mask you have been wearing all these years! A horrible painted mask!
You sold yourself for money. Oh! a common thief were better. You put yourself
up for sale to the highest bidder! You were bought in the market. You lied to the
whole world.

(*An Ideal Husband*, Act II)

Shaw too could be flat-footed when he was not offering epigrams;
this is Louka's exclamatory indignation:

You know how to hurt with your tongue as well as with your hands. But I dont
care, now Ive found out that whatever clay I'm made of, youre made of the
same. As for her, she's a liar; and her fine airs are a cheat; and I'm worth six of
her.

(*Arms and the Man*, Act II)

We get back to much more carefully contrived prose rhythms for
suggesting emotion-charged speech in Henry James's murder play,
*The Other House*, when Rose challenges the man who once loved her:

Didn't you come to see *where* I was? Didn't you come absolutely and publicly
*for* me? It was exactly when you found I was here that you did come back. You
had a perfect chance, on learning it, not to show; but you didn't take the chance –
you quickly put it aside. You reflected, you decided, you insisted we should
meet. I hadn't called you; I hadn't troubled you; I left you as perfectly alone as
I've *been* alone. It was your own passion and your own act – you've dropped on
me, you've overwhelmed me. You've overwhelmed me, I say, because I speak
from the depths of my surrender. But you didn't do it, I imagine, to be cruel,
and if you didn't do it to be cruel you did it to take what it could *give* you. You
know what I *am*, if *any* man has known, and it's to the thing I am – whatever that
is! – that you've come back at last from so far. It's the thing I am – whatever
that is! – that I count on you now to *stand by*.

(Act III)

In that speech there are deliberate repetitions of the same rhythm,
in fact of the same phrases, but they are interspersed with much more
varied rhythmical phrases, with an effect altogether less mechanical

than Wilde's speech for Lady Chilton. And yet it builds up to at least as much urgency, especially in the final '*stand by*', where the italicizing of both words gives a heavier stress than the ending of the previous sentence which is of almost the same rhythmical shape. The rhythm, naturally, is no more than an adjunct to the rhetoric of the sentences, but an important one.

This dialogue from older plays, with its crispness and its suggestion of tensely mobilized and discharged energy, uses entirely different rhythmical patterning from the low-key dialogue of many plays of the mid-twentieth century. There the skill has been to create rhythms that reinforce, in their very lack of force, the suggestion of low levels of motivation, uncertainty and loss of grip, the hint of a receding tide.

The approach I have suggested towards elucidating the expressive value of prose rhythm depends on viewing the movement of prose as analogous to gait and gesture and other bodily movements, with the constant transition from one posture to another that everyday activity presents. Like a person's movements, a writer's prose may have pleasing qualities, various in kind, slight or striking in degree, and not necessarily expressive of any attitude or mood; and we shall have our preferences among the ways in which people write as we do among the ways they hold themselves and move. Additionally, however, certain postures, gestures, and patterns of movement are expressive, and to some extent stand out from the continuous flow of movement which makes their context. The movement of a writer's prose similarly includes passages, short or long, frequent or infrequent, that appear to be expressive – of emotion, of mood, of relation to a person (peremptory, wheedling, etc.), or of approach to a situation (decisive, hesitant, jaunty, etc.). This last quality, I have suggested, is basic and probably underlies the others; it conveys the way in which energy is being spent, or ready to be spent – whether in a torrent or a trickle, with full determination or tentatively, in a controlled discharge or explosively, with dragging reluctance or eager zest, these among innumerable possibilities. It is in being an index of these 'energy' manifestations that rhythms accord with, and enhance, expressions of emotion and mood, the mournful, the gay, the fierce, for instance. But the sense of the language is needed too: if there is a language of rhythm alone it has a small vocabulary; each pattern of rhythm can be appropriate to a range of purposes one of which will be more narrowly defined by the sense of the words and the context. Nor – it scarcely needs saying – is there a simple 'code' of correspondences between a given rhythm wherever it occurs and an emotion; merely stating the idea is enough to rule it out for anyone who has a notion of the resources of language and the intricacies of their interrelation.

At present we have only subjective impressions, and the agreement about them which persuasive critics secure, to support the conviction that language rhythms are expressive. Experimental testing of the belief would not be impossible, but it would depend upon the fitness of the subjects for the experimental task required of them (a principle too often neglected in psychology); and it would present great difficulties if only because short, isolable language rhythms, however expressive in some contexts, are emotionally neutral in much of the ordinary flow of daily speech. It takes us a short step beyond complete subjectivity to examine the rhythms of fairly spontaneous utterance by competent writers, such as Dorothy Osborne and Benjamin Haydon, in contrasting emotional states. The greatest value of that exercise, however, lies in its compelling us to identify, in an objective way, the features of rhythm to which we attribute expressive effect; to have to make sure that what we are talking about is actually there puts at least some check on otherwise unanchored critical persuasiveness.

# 11

# The gist

Rhythmizing in language is an active process, not for the speaker or writer only but for the listener and reader as well. It is an active process of perceiving a unit, a whole, in a sequence of speech movements (perceived or imagined); syllabic runs and pauses, with differences of stress and duration among the syllables, define these wholes; and in the stream of language small units of rhythm may flow into one another, or may be kept disjunct by a well-marked pause ('But heark! / My pulse / ) or by a prolongation of sound ('like a soft Drum – Beats my approach. . .'), and in any case may contribute to a larger rhythmical whole. To speak of 'a rhythm' is like speaking of 'a form' in a painting, where a very large number of forms and their component sub-forms could if necessary be distinguished and only a small number are worth distinguishing.

Prose presents the chief problems of rhythm squarely, for it offers no temptation to rely on a fixed measuring rod with which to over-rule or support our perception of rhythmical units suggested by the runs, pauses and differential stressings of spoken English. And in prose 'a rhythm' is like 'a wave' of the sea which merges with larger wave movements and is itself almost always subdivisible into smaller wave forms if sufficiently close attention is given. In fact, as in so much perception, we create our own organized forms by ignoring the infinite gradations between one thing and another; we attend only to the bigger progressive steps, neglecting the 'ripples' or the 'choppy surface', calling the larger movements 'waves', and only occasionally observing how adjoining or successive waves are related to each other and how they all form part of the swell. It still remains perfectly sensible to speak of 'a wave' or 'a rhythm' as a distinguishable, although not isolated, unit.

The literary significance of rhythm and rhythms can best be understood by regarding language movement (created by the muscles at work in speech or imagined in silent reading) as comparable to such systems of bodily movement as walking, gesture, and patterns of changing posture. Like these it can be described in terms of broad characteristics – flowing, jerky, patterned, disjointed, and so on – which give rise to similarly broad aesthetic appraisals, the total effect being in some degree pleasing or unpleasing, and described in such terms as graceful, charming, harmonious, clumsy, affected, unlovely. These very broad judgements rapidly pass into something more specifically descriptive; words like lively, sluggish, solemn, impressive, playful, emphatic, sombre, lighthearted, peremptory, hesitant, will begin to imply the expressive effects of particular rhythmical patterns, some referring to mood and emotion, and others to the attitude of the writer or his personae towards those he addresses, towards the situation he faces, or towards his themes and topics.

There is always the risk of attributing to rhythm an expressive significance that stems in reality from other features of language. The sense of the words, and the intonation (or pattern of pitch changes) in which the sense is reflected, are the factors most likely to produce effects with which rhythm is mistakenly credited; but the tempo of the reading and the variations of tempo, the accelerations and slowings, also have an effect, as does the quality of voice with which the sounds are attacked. The interaction of these and no doubt other features of language will often make it difficult to identify the particular contribution of rhythm, but it seems reasonably certain that rhythm in itself has potential expressive value which will become effective when other factors favour it. Differences in the length of rhythm units, whether they flow into one another or are more clearly disjunct, the suddenness of change from one stress pattern to another, the differences between units composed largely of heavy stresses and those with a rapid run of lightly stressed syllables, the cumulative effect of a succession of broadly similar rhythmical units, the rhythmical addendum to what offers itself as a completed unit – these possibilities among others, and in endless combinations, help in themselves to convey such qualities of action as surprise, hesitancy or conflict, flowing ease, conviction, impetuosity, forceful determination, wavering uncertainty, disengaged lightness of touch, crisp finality.

These are modes of energy expenditure (or of preparedness for expending it) and are not sharply delimited from one another. We need not wonder how the rhythm comes to 'express' them; it is part of them.

They themselves form part of the total emotional response, if that is taken as meaning the evaluative response arising when an event, a person, an idea is recognized as relevant to the structure of interests and sentiments – the structure of values – of the given reader. The emotional response is the way a situation is evaluated in relation both to the sentiments of the person facing it and to his resources for coping with it. It may, for instance, be disagreeable and terrifying, disagreeable and angering, delightful and offering effortless enjoyment, delightful and demanding eager seizure, or amusing, disgusting, giving relief, creating anxiety or suspense, and so on, through the innumerable shades of 'feeling' we can experience about an event, a person, an occasion. It is the energy aspect of the response which the rhythm can suggest or enhance. The sense of the words is needed before we know whether a forceful rhythm is suggesting eager joy, determination, anger or horror, and whether a languid movement is helping to convey romantic yearning or sadness or resignation or quiet relief. These are no more than rough indications – far removed from the subtlety and complexity of serious literature.

No sharp line can be drawn between a directly perceptible unit of rhythm and those larger movement patterns in prose – a cumulative paragraph, for example – which may become evident only on retrospection. Individual readers will to some extent differ in the amount they can organize into a rhythmical unit, and for each person the amount will vary a little with his familiarity with the particular material and with his increasing skill as a reader. But though there is no sharp dividing line the distinction remains valid and the extremes are readily discriminated – at one extreme the rhythm which is an immediate fact of perception, at the other the movement structure of a long section of prose which can be identified only when we reflect and look back. In fine prose the two forms of organization are mutually enhancing.

The difference between prose and verse is that the line, which in prose is only a typographical necessity to be ignored in reading, becomes in verse a rhythmical unit; at the same time the line ending is given value as a special form of punctuation. The line is made up of a number of smaller units of rhythm – occasionally of a single unit – and in a line of several rhythmical sub-units there is likely to be a point of slight pause, the caesura, which gives the line two rhythmical parts. The form taken by the sub-units, and the extent to which the caesura is marked, always conform to natural speech rhythm (except for special effects, chiefly facetious – 'And now he is the ruler of the Queen's Navee'). In free verse the dominance of natural speech is unmistakable. In metrical verse, where a rhythmical pattern is repeated fairly closely, perhaps several times, and establishes a set for rhythmizing succeeding groups of syllables in the same form, the metre will determine which out of more than one possible speech rhythm is adopted. But if the metre and an inescapable speech rhythm conflict, the speech rhythm takes precedence. When prosodists find the result rhythmically acceptable they call the deviation from metre a permissible licence; when unacceptable, a metrical fault.

A more adequate account of rhythm should be able to explain why, simply as a group of speech movements, a particular set of syllables seems unacceptable in its syllabic context. This is a crux, commonly evaded and not easily resolved. A first step towards a solution lies in recognizing that the verse line is a rhythmical unit and that therefore its sub-units must be in some sense compatible with each other. Compatibility does not imply uniformity of stress pattern, nor does it require that each unit should flow smoothly out of and into the adjacent units – there may be rhythmical disjunctions, pauses between one unit and the next, and still the line be experienced as a coherent whole. Nor, again, is the sequential pattern of strong and weak stresses a decisive factor: it is possible to show that the same sequence of strong and weak stresses can, with different words, give a unified or a disjointed line; the difference lies in the units of speech rhythm into which the same sequence of differentiated stresses is divided.

The prosodists always had a comfortable non-answer to the question of unsatisfactory rhythms: it was merely asserted that such and such 'feet' could not be satisfactorily combined. This was simply a labelling of certain rhythms which, when adjacent, break the rhythmical unity of the line. It left unasked the question *why* they will not satisfactorily combine in a verse line despite the fact that they may run together easily enough in prose. The answer seems to be that a disjointed effect occurs when part of the line establishes a firm set to which another part of the line will not conform. This is not just a way of saying that the line must be 'regular'. An extremely irregular line – for instance, 'High birth, vigour of bone, desert in service' – has a satisfying unity which depends on the very fact that it *is* irregular, and that no part of it creates a strong enough set to disturb us as we pass from one rhythmical sub-unit to another of quite different stress patterning. Successful free verse, too, has to avoid setting up a repetitive pattern in one part of a line and disrupting it in another; a succession of dissimilar speech rhythms can be unified, but an invitation to regular movement offered at one point, only to be withdrawn at another, brings stumbling and a disjointed line.

No simple formula will predict whether the rhythms offered at one point in a line are strongly enough marked to establish a set to which we try to conform throughout the line. The rhythmical set in reading is too flexible to allow its limits to be simply defined. It is like the steps we take in going down one of those roughly made stairway paths on a cliff or a steep slope: a few successive treads will be sufficiently similar to set up a pattern of movement, but they will be followed by others so unequal in length that the pattern is disrupted and we have to shorten our stride unnaturally, or lengthen it, or take two strides on one tread.

The fact that a verse line can be unacceptable simply in its syllabic sequences presents a difficult problem. There are quite other kinds of unsatisfactory rhythm, more easily understood in principle although identifiable as unsatisfactory only by still more subjective judgement. To begin with, the general 'aesthetic' characteristics of a passage of verse or prose may be disagreeable: its monotony, jerkiness, flaccidity, heavyfootedness, for instance. Secondly, the expressive value of a rhythm or sequence of rhythms may be inappropriate, in the kind of energy-deployment it suggests, to the emotions conveyed by the sense and associations of the words. Thirdly, the syllabic runs and pauses of the speech rhythms may at times obscure the mere sense of the words; sense unit and rhythm unit can occasionally conflict.

The validity of any appraisal of rhythm on these three grounds must depend on the sensitiveness of the reader, it can always be challenged by other readers, it will always be to some extent influenced by fashion. It shares these limitations with any literary appraisal. But the notions of aesthetically pleasing or unpleasing language movement, of incongruity between the feelings conveyed by the sense and by the rhythm, and of dislocation between sense unit and rhythm unit are, as general principles, fairly simple.

In recapitulating my argument I have reversed the order of presentation, working backwards from prose and irregular verse towards metrical rhythms. This is less misleading than the conventional route (taken for instance by Saintsbury) of beginning with something as specialized and contrived as regular metre, making concessions to its deviations and licences, and then seeking in prose a diluted or modified form of the intense rhythmical organization of verse. It is from rhythms inherent in the natural speaking of the language that all rhythmical writing begins. In strict metrical verse speech rhythms have been selected in a way that produces successive repetitions of the same movement pattern, or the same combination of patterns. The regularity of repetition is seldom complete (being intolerably tedious if it is); the natural rhythms of the spoken language take precedence and will disturb the metre if they conflict with it. When conflict between speech rhythm and metre does occur there is no 'compromise'; the metre is broken, or more commonly bent a little. The fact is that the metres used by serious poets bear little resemblance to the simple patterns which prosodists identify and, having identified, proceed to disintegrate with 'permissible deviations'. The 'set' established by a metrical scheme, which makes us ready for a certain range of coming rhythms but not others, is fairly broad or flexible, and the factors that establish it in a given poem may be much less simple than the repeated stress pattern of a standard metre.

Serious verse, even in a form as seemingly strict as the line of Dryden and Pope, is an organization of diverse rhythms, not the repetition of metrical feet. For this reason alone – and there are others – the suggestion that metrical verse works through some hypnoidal effect would be highly improbable. It remains true of much verse, however, that the metrical scheme, the stanza form (with perhaps short and long lines in a prescribed pattern), and often a rime scheme as well, produce so many constraints that to achieve sense, speech rhythm, and grammatical structure within them demands a high level of skill which can give pleasure in itself. This is the superadded attraction of metrical writing that Wordsworth respected. It deserves respect, like other decorative arts, but it can in an extreme form produce something of the lulling effect that the hypnoidal theory of metre would explain; the ingenious patternings of some of the Elizabethan lyrics, or the simultaneously fascinating and soothing effect of the repetitive swing, resourcefully varied in detail, of Swinburne's verse may tempt us to attend too little to the sense and values the poem offers, and to miss lapses (or occasionally masterly condensations) of sense, and false notes of feeling. Fashions in verse and criticism fluctuate in the amount of attention given to the 'formal' aspects of poetry, including its metrical patterning, compared with the attention claimed by its sense and its organization of feeling. When these latter form the focus of interest, rhythm is likely to count for more than any metrical scheme based on repetition.

The abstract arguments and simple illustrative examples I have offered are necessarily at a far remove from the literary realities and subtleties that sensitive reading recognizes. Compared with the effects I have examined, the full influence of rhythm in writing is more various, more delicately shaded, more complex in its interaction with the sense of phrases and their wider context, more intimately affected by other features of the sound of words. But an abstract framework can serve a useful purpose if it is broad enough, and accurate enough as far as it goes, not to distort or cramp the finer perceptions and discriminations. The rhythm of language which helps to express the most ordinary feelings of everyday life is equally one element among the immeasurable resources of the greatest writing. With or without theory, any sensitive and practised reading must be responsive to it. Only when, as critics or in discussion with friends, we want to identify the rhythmical aspect of what we perceive, and describe its effect, do we feel the need for intelligible terms and believable explanations. It is these that I have been trying to find.

# References

Abbott, C. C., *The Life and Letters of George Darley: Poet and Critic*, Oxford, 1967 (1st ed. 1928)

Abercrombie, David, *Studies in Phonetics and Linguistics*, London, 1965

Allen, W. Sidney, *Accent and Rhythm: Prosodic Features in Latin and Greek: A Study in Theory and Reconstruction*, Cambridge, 1973

Allen, W. Stannard, *Living English Speech: Stress and Intonation Practice for Foreign Students*, London, 1954

Attridge, Derek, *Well-Weighed Syllables: Elizabethan Verse in Classical Metres*, Cambridge, 1974

Brasch, Charles, *Ambulando*, Christchurch, New Zealand, 1964

Brown, Peter, *Augustine of Hippo*, London, 1967

Chatman, Seymour, *A Theory of Meter*, The Hague, 1964

Chisholm, A. R., '*La Pythie* and its place in Valéry's work', *Modern Language Review*, LVIII, 1; January 1963

Classe, André, *The Rhythm of English Prose*, Oxford (Blackwell), 1939

Croll, Morris W., 'The rhythm of English verse', 1929; 'The cadence of English oratorical prose', 1919; in *Style, Rhetoric and Rhythm: Essays by Morris W. Croll*, ed. J. Max Patrick *et al.*, Princeton, 1966

Darley, George, *see* Abbott, C. C.

Daunt, Marjorie, 'Old English verse and English speech rhythms', *Transactions of the Philological Society*, 1946

Davies, J. B., 'New tests of musical aptitude', *Brit. J. Psychology*, 62, 4; November 1971

Davis, N., *Paston Letters and Papers of the Fifteenth Century*, Oxford, 1971

Deighton, K., Arden edition of *Troilus and Cressida*, London, 1906

Dickens, Charles, *The Letters of Charles Dickens*, ed. M. House and G. Storey, Oxford, 1965

Eells, George, *The Life that Late he Led: a Biography of Cole Porter*, London, 1967

Eliot, T. S., *The Use of Poetry and the Use of Criticism*, London, 1933
*The Music of Poetry*, Glasgow, 1942
*Poetry and Drama*, London, 1951

Gillham, D. G., *Blake's Contrary States*, Cambridge, 1966

Greene, D. H. and Stephens, E. M., *J. M. Synge*, New York, 1959

Gwynn, F. L., Condee, R. W., Lewis, A. O. Jr., *The Case for Poetry: a Critical Anthology* (2nd ed.), New Jersey, 1965

Halle, M. and Keyser, S. J., *English Stress: Its Form, Its Growth, and Its Role in Verse*, New York, 1971

Harding, D. W., 'Rhythmization and speed of work', *Brit. J. Psychology*, XXIII, 3; January 1933

    'The rhythmical intention in Wyatt's poetry', *Scrutiny*, XIV, 2; December 1946

Haydon, B. R., *The Diary of Benjamin Robert Haydon*, ed. W. B. Pope, Cambridge, Mass., 1963

H. D., *Sea Garden*, London, 1916

Holloway, John, *The Charted Mirror*, London, 1960

Hough, Graham, *Image and Experience*, London, 1960

Ing, Catherine, *Elizabethan Lyrics*, London, 1951

James, H. E. O., ' 'Regularity and rhythmicalness', *Brit. J. Psychology*, XVII, 1; July 1926

Jameson, Storm (ed.) *London Calling*, New York and London, 1942

Keyser, S. J., *see* Halle, M. and Keyser, S. J.

Knights, L. C., *Explorations*, London, 1946

    'Early Blake', in *Explorations* 3, London, 1976

Langer, Susanne K., *Feeling and Form*, London, 1953

Lawrence, D. H., *Birds, Beasts and Flowers*, London, 1923

    *The Letters of D. H. Lawrence*, ed. Aldous Huxley, London, 1932

Leavis, F. R., *New Bearings in English Poetry*, London, 1932

    *Revaluation*, London, 1936

Lewis, C. S., 'The fifteenth century heroic line', *English Association Essays and Studies*, 1938

Lowell, Robert, *Life Studies*, New York, 1959

MacDougall, R., 'Structure of simple rhythm forms', *Psychological Monographs*, IV, 17; 1903

Mayor, J. B., *Chapters on English Metre*, Cambridge, 1901

Miner, J. B., 'Motor, visual and applied rhythms', *Psychological Monographs*, V, 4; 1903

Moore, J., *The Life and Letters of Edward Thomas*, London, 1939

Moore, Marianne, *Selected Poems*, London, 1935

Morley, John, 'Macaulay in *Critical Miscellanies: Second Series*, London, 1877

Munro, C. K., *Watching a Play*, London, 1933

Murphy, Gardner, *An Historical Introduction to Modern Psychology*, London, 1932

Oliver, H. J., New Arden edition of *Timon of Athens*, London, 1959

Omond, T. S., *A Study of Metre*, London, 1903

Osborne, Dorothy, *The Letters of Dorothy Osborne to William Temple*, ed. G. C. Moore Smith, Oxford, 1928

Ostriker, Alicia, *Vision and Verse in William Blake*, Madison and Milwaukee, Wisconsin, 1965

Pike, Kenneth L., *The Intonation of American English*, Ann Arbor, 1945

Pope, J. C., *The Rhythm of Beowulf*, New Haven, 1942

Read, Herbert, *Education Through Art*, London, 1943

Richards, I. A., *Principles of Literary Criticism*, London, 1926

    *Practical Criticism*, London, 1929

Ridler, Anne, in Rajan, B. (ed.), *T. S. Eliot: a Study of his Writing by Several Hands*, London, 1947

Robinson, Ian, *Chaucer's Prosody: A Study of the Middle English Verse Tradition*, Cambridge, 1971

Saintsbury, George, *History of English Prosody*, London, 1908

'Prosody from Chaucer to Spenser' in *Cambridge History of English Literature*, vol. III, Cambridge, 1908

*History of English Prose Rhythm*, London, 1912

Sherrington, C. S., *The Integrative Action of the Nervous System*, New Haven, 1906

Southall, Raymond, *The Courtly Maker*, Oxford (Blackwell), 1964

Speirs, John, 'A survey of medieval verse', *Pelican Guide to English Literature*, ed. B. Ford, vol. I, Harmondsworth, 1954

Stetson, R. H., *Motor Phonetics: a Study of Speech Movements in Action* (2nd ed.), Amsterdam, 1951

Stoffel, Cornelis, *see* Van Damm and Stoffel

Sutherland, James, *The Medium of Poetry*, London, 1934

Synge, J. M., *Poems and Translations*, Churchtown, 1909

Thomas, Edward, *see* Moore, J.

Thompson, John, *The Founding of English Metre*, London, 1961

Thomson, William, *The Rhythm of Speech*, Glasgow, 1923

Tillyard, E. M. W., *Poetry Direct and Oblique*, London, 1934

Trager, George L. and Smith Jr., Henry Lee, 'An outline of English structure', *Studies in Linguistics, Occasional Papers*, 3, Norman, Oklahoma, 1951

Trickett, Rachel, *The Honest Muse*, Oxford, 1967

Van Damm, B. A. P. and Stoffel, Cornelis, *Chapters on English Printing, Prosody and Pronunciation 1550–1700*, Heidelberg, 1902

Ward, James, *Psychological Principles*, Cambridge, 1918

Wilson, J. Dover, The Cambridge Edition of *The Tempest*, Cambridge, 1921

# Index

Page numbers in italics refer to passages quoted for illustration or analysis. Well-known works cited or quoted in the text without the author's name are indexed under the author.

Abbott, C. C., 29
Abercrombie, David, 8, 93, 117
Addison, Joseph, 124
Aldington, Richard, 56
Allen, W. Sidney, 11
Allen, W. Stannard, 9–12, 134
Arnold, Matthew, *12–13*, 99
Attridge, Derek, 11
Augustine, St, 98
Austen, Jane, *138–9*

Bale, John, *62*
Barclay, Alexander, 59
Bartholomew Fair, 102
Baxter, Richard, 69
Beardsley, M., 32
Blake, William, *3*, *34–5*, *91–2*, 97
Bolton, T. L., 5
*Book of Common Prayer*, 121
Bottomley, Gordon, 23
Brasch, Charles, 69
Bridges, Robert, 32
Brown, Peter, 98
Browne, Sir Thomas, 18, *124*
Browning, Robert, *26–7*, 55
Burke, Edmund, *127*
Burnet, Bishop, 25
Burrows, Abe, 87
Burton, Robert, *125*, *140*
Byron, Lord, 29

Chatman, Seymour, 31–2, 34
Chaucer, Geoffrey, 11, 59, 60–1, *62–3*
Chaucerians, Scottish, 61, 63
Chisholm, A. R., 87
Clarke, C. Cowden, 53
Classe, André, 116–17

Coleridge, S. T., 29, 97, *104*
Congreve, William, *148–9*
Connolly, Cyril, *131*
Conrad, Joseph, *13–14*
Croll, Morris W., 19–20, 96, 121–3, 124, 125, 134, 138, 139

Dalcroze, Jacques, 2
dancing, 96
Darley, George, 28
Daunt, Marjorie, 17, 18, 22
Davies, J. B., 9–10
Davis, N., 73
Deighton, K., 53
Dickens, Charles, *48*, *135*, 137
Donne, John, 3, *26*, *33*, 106, *108*, 136
Drayton, Michael, *37*, 55
Dryden, John, 3, 25, *101*, *105–6*, *110*, 157

*Edward IV*, 60
Eells, George, 87
Eliot, T. S., *14*, 24, 56, 57–8, 70, *78–9*, *80–1*, 82, 83, 86–7, *88–9*, 94, *95–6*, 99, *111*, *112*
Ellis-Fermor, Una, 79
emotional states, 100–2, 154
English speech rhythms, 12–14

Fitzgerald, Edward, *21*
Flecker, James Elroy, 100
Florio, John, *63–4*
Forbes, Mansfield D., 97
Frost, Robert, 22, 23, *45–7*

Gibbon, Edward, *123*, *139*
Gilbert, W. S., *155*
Gillham, D. G., *91–2*

Greene, D. H., 142
Greene, Robert, 66
Gregory, Lady, 141
Greville, Fulke, *119–20*
Grove, A. P., 77
Gwynn, F. L. et al., 4
Halle, M., 32, 34, 43
Hanmer, Sir Thomas, 55
Harding, D. W., 7, 59
Hardy, Thomas, *25, 47, 110*
Harvey, C. J. D., 77
Hawes, Stephen, 59, *62*
Haydon, B. R., *146–8*, 151
H. D., *67*
Henley, W. E., *99*
Herbert, George, 83
Herrick, Robert, 83, *111*
Heywood, John, *62*
Holloway, John, 17, 18, 22
Hood, Thomas, *98–9*, 143
Hooker, Richard, 118, 124
Hopkins, Gerard Manley, *23–4*, 29, *64–6*, 106
Hough, Graham, 67–8, 70
Hyde, Douglas, 142

Ibsen, Henrik, 136
imagist poets, 18, 67
Ing, Catherine, 19–22, 37, 49–50, 107
intonation, 16, 34, 89–91, 113, 139

James, Henry, *137–8, 149–50*
James, H. E. O., 15
Jameson, Storm, 78
Johnson, Samuel, 39, 147

Kean, Edmund, 28–9
Kemble, J. P., 28–9
Keyser, S. J., 32, 34, 43
King, Henry, *105, 110, 152*
Knights, L. C., 3, 87, 89, 105, 107

Langer, Susanne, 2
Langland, William, *61*, 66
Lawrence, D. H., *68*, 99–100
Leavis, F. R., 3, 23, 133
Lewis, C. S., 17
Locke, John, *125–6*, 130, 133
Longfellow, H. W., 55
Lowell, Robert, *68*
Lydgate, John, 60
Lyly, John, 119

Macaulay, Lord, 18, 141
Macdougall, R., 5

McGonagall, William, 72
Marsh, Edward, 99
Marvell, Andrew, *41–2*
Mayor, J. B., 36
metre
  and 'counterpoint', 39, 44, 45–8, 65
  expectation and set, 40–4, 45–9, 82–3
  the foot, 32–3, 53, 65–6, 77, 155
  'hypnotic effects', 85–6, 157
  iambic, 27–9, 32–4, 43, 50–1, 53–5, 60, 97
  lapses, 72
  licences, 17, 31–2, 41, 64, 74, 83, 155, 157
  as superadded attraction, 49–50, 158
Milton, John, 23, *35*, 65, 83, 99, 123
Miner, J. B., 5
*Mirror for Magistrates*, 60
Montaigne, Michel de, 63–4
mood, 100, 150
Moore, J., 23
Moore, Marianne, *69–70*
Moore, T. Sturge, 22
Morley, John, 141
morse code, 10–11
Munro, C. K., 136
Muir, Kenneth, 89
Murphy, Gardner, 125
Myers, L. H., *132*

Neail, Marianne, 28
Noyes, Alfred, *93*

Occleve, Thomas, 60
Oliver, H. J., 79
Omond, T. S., 19, 20
Osborne, Dorothy, *143–5*, 148, 151
Ostriker, Alicia, 34

Paston Letters, *73–4*
Petrarch, 142
Pike, Kenneth L., 117
Poe, Edgar Allan, *98*
Pope, Alexander, 24, *27–8, 112*, 157
Pope, J. C., 35–6
Pope, W. B., 146
Porter, Cole, 87
Pound, Ezra, *109–10*
prose
  isochronous intervals, 116–18
  cadences, 86, 121–3, 138, 139
  metrical feet in, 119–21, 127
  metrical intrusions, 128–9
  'sectional', 127
  in Shakespeare, 127–30

and speech, 126–7, 148
'utilitarian', 124, 125–7, 131–3
prosody, 31–6, 60
Psalms, 83

Read, Herbert, 2
rhythm
  aesthetic value, 123–4, 141–2, 153
  of 'afterthought', 138–9
  in creative process, 86–9
  definition, 5–6
  and emotion, 98–9, 100, 140–1, 150–1
  and energy, 101–4, 107–10, 114, 139–40,
    150, 154
  expressive, 72, 92–7, 98–115, 124–5,
    119, 134, 136–51, 153–4
  flowing, 12–16, 59–65, 82, 104, 123, 155
  as a Gestalt, 15
  imitative, 93–6
  and movement, 104–5, 107–8, 110, 140
  notation, 9, 134–5
  of paragraph, 66, 88, 135–6, 154
  and regular repetition, 22, 82
  revisions by poets, 88–9
  'running' and 'sprung', 64–6
  in speech, 7–9
  of speech as movement system, 92–3,
    96–7, 114, 141, 150, 153
  of speech in verse, 17–18, 22–30, 34–9,
    155, 157
  and 'structure', 136–7
  subjective, 5, 15
  and syntax, 133, 147, 156–7
  in typewriting, 6–7
  units in speech, 12, 66, 76, 104, 120,
    144–5, 147, 152, 155
  unsatisfactory, 72–84, 131–3, 155–6
Richards, I. A., 4, 5, 45, 123
Ridler, Anne, 94
Robinson, F. N., 60
Robinson, Ian, 25, 26, 59
Rosenberg, Isaac, 81, 83, 93–4
Rowe, N., 55
Royal Society, 125

Saintsbury, George, 5, 60–2, 74, 77, 81,
  83, 118–21, 122, 123–5, 127, 130–1,
  134, 140, 141, 157
scansion, 53, 113–14, 119–21
Shakespeare, William, 18, 21, 26, 28–9,
  37–9, 47, 50–7, 58, 59, 70, 74, 75,
  79–80, 83, 84, 89–91, 100, 105, 106,
  109, 110, 112, 127–30
Shaw, G. B., 149
Shelley, Percy Bysshe, 56, 103–4

Sherrington, Sir Charles, 131–3
Shirley, Henry, 74–6, 77
Shirley, James, 81
Sidney, Sir Philip, 11, 106
Skelton, John, 17
Smith, Jr., Henry Lee, 9, 11
Smith, G. C. Moore, 143
Southall, Raymond, 59, 106–7
Speirs, John, 63
Spenser, Edmund, 11
Sprat, Thomas, 125
Steevens, G., 39
Stephens, E. M., 142
Stetson, R. H., 92
Stoffel, Cornelis, 51
Suckling, Sir John, 83
Surrey, Earl of, 59
Sutherland, James, 97, 101
Swinburne, Charles Algernon, 25–6, 40–3,
  49, 73, 74, 86, 120, 158
syllable
  duration, 9–11, 80
  quantity, 11
  stress, 8–9, 92–3
Symonds, J. A., 36
Synge, J. M., 141–3

Temple, Sir William, 121, 124, 144–5
tempo, 16, 34
Tennyson, Lord, 35–6, 47–8, 63, 74
Thomas, Edward, 23, 107–8, 114
Thompson, John, 35, 59, 60, 61
Thomson, William, 9, 19, 20, 28, 31, 35–6,
  53
Tottel's Miscellany, 50, 53, 59
Tillyard, E. M. W., 4
Trager, George L., 9, 11
Trickett, Rachel, 3

Valéry, Paul, 87
Van Damm, B. A. P., 51
Van Wyck Louw, N. P., 76–7
verse
  caesura in, 56–7, 61, 74–5
  free, 66–71, 156
  isochronous intervals in, 18–22
  line, 67–71, 72, 78, 79, 82–3, 111–12,
    154–5
  line ending, 69, 80–2, 110–13
  Middle English, 17, 59, 61–3
  Old English, 18, 59–60
  quantitative, 11
  syllabic, 63–4
  in theatre, 83–4
Villon, François, 142

Waller, Lewis, 28
Ward, James, 5, 15
*Weep you no more, sad fountains*, 19–20
Wells, Rulon, 32
Whitman, Walt, 83
Wilde Oscar, *149*, 150
Wilson, John Dover, 51–3
Wimsatt, W. K., 32

Woolf, Virginia, 87
Wordsworth, William, 50, *97*, 98–9, *102–3*, *107*, 158
Wyatt, Sir Thomas, 17, 59, 60, *63*, 106, *107*

Yeats, W. B., *112–14*
Young, C. M., 29